Flight to Reliability
Proven Principles for
High-Reliability Success
Jeffrey Harvey P.E.

Apollo Digital Group LLC

ISBN 979-8-9866340-7-4 (Paperback)
ISBN 979-8-9866340-8-1 (Ebook)

Publisher: Apollo Digital Group LLC
www.jeffreyharveype.com

Contents

Free Giveaways

www.jeffreyharveype.com

Introduction

One earnest worker can do more by personal suggestion to prevent accidents than a carload of safety signs. –E. R Brown

Complex operations come with inherent risks. Yet despite this complexity, some organizations seem to operate reliably and repeatedly with little to no catastrophic incidents. For a while, it wasn't exactly clear how this could be achieved, but through careful study of their operations, we now have a blueprint for transforming any organization into a high-reliability organization. Everything is based on the mindset surrounding the operations and how each part of the operation relates to the human element. Reliable operations result in products and processes that are safe and reliable to the frontline worker as well as the public. A crucial piece of the puzzle is managers who understand that violations of public safety have consequences for an organization's finances, reputation, and future. Managers act as the link between operations on the ground and organizational policy. This makes managers in high-risk organizations the ultimate custodians of public safety. Both managers and executives are expected to be competent to guarantee that their products and services remain safe regardless of the risks associated. Furthermore, the rules and regulations that high-risk operations are subject to play a significant role in ensuring that safety protocols are observed, but what ultimately sets such organizations apart from the rest of the field is the exceptional safety culture ingrained across all aspects of their business operations.

The airline industry as a whole is one example of a complex operation that has been consistently reliable over the years. From the coordination between air traffic control and pilots to the complexity of the aircraft itself, it is surprising that air travel is the safest mode of transport (Turbli, 2022). The cultural standards in this industry have numerous painful lessons for them to develop into what we see today. For this reason, it is beneficial to use examples from aviation-related operations and incidents to explain the principles of HROs. Moreover, the industry, while complex, has a simple relationship between different levels of authority, hence this book's reliance on it to explain high-reliability organization (HRO) concepts.

Transforming an organization into an HRO is half the job. Maintaining a safety culture is also paramount; otherwise, an organization can quickly lose its reliability status and the safety or profitability that comes with this reliability. One example highlighting the importance of a superior safety culture to maintain a high-reliability organization is the two tragic crashes of the Boeing 737 Max 8 months after the aircraft was introduced into commercial service. At first, it appeared that the first crash was just an accident. Professional opinions quickly changed after the second crash as the evidence pointed to a systematic problem with either the product or the company's safety culture. Soon enough, the public began to question the company's products, and the subsequent investigations verifying the mistakes made by the company cost the company dearly. The top management left, and the company had to pay over $2 billion in fines. This is a staggering amount of money that can cripple an organization, and smaller organizations cannot afford to make such mistakes. Engineering professionals, particularly those with managerial roles, must stay clear of similar mistakes, especially when the expectation is that more highly reliable organizations will be needed in the future. Managers in charge of operations within their organizations need to learn how to turn their organizations into HROs.

By definition, HROs are high-risk organizations where errors rarely occur at any stage of the business operations. The goal is zero harm because should something go wrong, the outcome is likely to be catastrophic to human life. Good engineering practice is at the core of the quality and reliability that HROs are able to deliver consistently. The challenge is that transforming an organization into an HRO is easier said than done, and maintaining this transformation demands a certain set of skills and competencies from mid-level managers and an equal commitment from the executives. These are the drivers to ensure that the principles behind the success of HROs are maintained and considerable financial resources are needed. We will discuss these principles in detail starting from the third chapter, relating these to where Boeing and other organizations failed, but also including organizations or operations that have consistently got it right. General employees play a significant role, too, since they are on the frontlines to alert managers on the potential sources of problems, among other things. This means that everyone within the organization is a stakeholder in this cultural shift and must be empowered for the transformation to work.

Since high-reliability organizations are complex and challenging to maintain, it's unsurprising that a number of STEM managers do not know how to operationalize such organizations. This knowledge gap has been the main motivation for writing this book, with the ultimate goal being to teach managers within high-risk organizations how to be competent in mapping such organizations. Many of the lessons presented in this book are based on professional experience and the knowledge acquired throughout my career spanning over 20 years. Managers in high-risk environments such as nuclear power and chemical processing plants will benefit the most from this book and will learn how to manage the complex, dynamic, and unexpected situations that might arise in their daily operations, particularly when new systems are introduced.

One of my favorite principles among the five is "preoccupation with failure" because of its relevance to new systems. It is also the starting point for new managers and graduate engineers to build their approach to HROs because it opens the door for the remaining principles to be learned. New systems and processes always carry an added risk to the company's operations because things do not always turn out as expected. I found this to be true during the early stages of my career. During that time, the organization I was employed by built a new facility with the goal of increasing the production rate. In the beginning, it appeared that everything worked well. However, as soon as the output began to approach the design level, the facility became unstable, leading to products that were outside the specifications, which resulted in significant "off-specification" fines for the company, costing around $1 million each month. This was expensive and unsustainable for the company, and a solution needed to be found. There were many theories surrounding the cause of the problem, and both internal and external engineering teams were persistent in their efforts to find the cause of the problem. After weeks of trial and error, the problem was narrowed down to the vessel, and the chances of getting the problem solved looked bleak. Many organizations face a similar dilemma when new systems are introduced. Given the choice to continue pursuing a solution or have the facility operate at a lower output, what option would you take?

The Road to Reliability

As we move along, we will address the mindset you need to approach similar decisions, starting off with introducing the origins of high-reliability organizations, what they are, and the five principles that make HROs work. The principles are preoccupation with failure, sensitivity to operations, deference to expertise, commitment to resilience, and reluctance to simplify. These principles do not work under the assumption that nothing will go wrong. Instead, they ensure that in the event that something does go wrong, there is no serious danger to the public or other critical things that affect reliability. From this book, managers can expect to gain knowledge essential for leading their organizations toward exhibiting all the characteristics of HROs, with the end goal being a low accident or failure rate. This means that the processes specific to the organization must reduce the occurrence and impact of catastrophic failures.

Fortunately, today's industries have more data to get deeper insights. This wasn't the case at the beginning of my career, and more work was needed to make sure that organizations remained reliable. In this regard, there will be an emphasis on the importance of data, which is critical when it comes to training employees or deciding on the interventions needed for course correction. This should translate into reliability and streamlined life-critical forms. If implemented correctly, organizations can expect reduced administrative work and cost burden to their organizations when it comes to work management and failure avoidance. Read on to learn how to keep your organization reliable and your products safe. With that said, let us begin our journey of understanding how high-reliability organizations work.

Chapter 1

Origins of High-Reliability Organizations

It will never happen to me. –Captain E. J Smith

High-reliability organizations, or HROs, are a relatively new area for mainstream industries. To get to where we are today, it took a series of disasters, accidents, and the relevant human responses to these events for researchers to begin seriously looking into HROs. The sinking of the Titanic is one example of a disaster that paved the way for public safety to be an important matter for both lawmakers and organizations. This and other events piqued the interest of several researchers, with the focus gradually shifting to the causes of disasters. Perhaps an important book on this subject is *Normal Accidents* by Charles Perrow (1999). According to the findings, when organizations are really complicated, and things are connected tightly together, there is a likelihood that big accidents will happen even from small errors. This is more pronounced when there is a lack of coordination in managing the processes, either in production or during operations. Further work by James Short and Lee Clarke determined that when accidents or mistakes happen due to errors, it is rarely one individual's fault (Roberts, 2003). The argument is that for an organization to be reliable, a collective approach is needed because major errors or the collection of small errors is never the fault of a single individual.

This can easily be related to the sinking of the Titanic. The common story is that the ship sank because it hit an iceberg. Modern evidence suggests that there was more to this disaster. One finding is that the ship was traveling too fast in icy waters, meaning the actual operation was unsafe, and the crew was insensitive to operations. Other factors included poor coordination, leading to the ship taking a wrong turn to head for the iceberg instead of away from it (Tikkanen, 2023). The final and most important reason is that the ship's maker attempted to cut costs to produce the ship. The rivets holding the hull plates contained slag in high concentrations, which could have weakened the area that hit the iceberg. Of course, mass transportation had not reached the scale we see in the modern day, and luxury was more important than safety. Over time, organizations in high-risk industries began to develop a culture that was directed towards safe outcomes as companies understood the legal, ethical, and business implications of poor safety practices or systems.

The crash of United Airlines 173 paved the way for airlines to start adopting the early versions of principles on which HROs are founded. It was already understood that accidents rarely happen because of one simple reason, and the research that went into this focused on team building, which ultimately resulted in what is now known as Crew Resource Management (CRM) in the airline industry. The idea is to leverage the redundancies that must be naturally built into complex systems, products, and processes where people are involved. This is the foundation of what we see as reliability, and this idea of high-reliability organizations evolved over time, eventually expanding into other industries. In the 1990s, the US Coast Guard adopted HRO principles when it introduced its "Prevention through People" program, which is monitored by outsiders who assess the program regularly to guarantee safe and reliable operations. The banking sector is another example, particularly the SWIFT interbank system, which has its "failure is not an option" program built using HRO principles (Roberts, 2003). Across the board, the bulk of the progress was made as technology advanced and people started to learn and understand the large-scale implications of risky operations. It seemed everyone wanted an organization that was reliable simply because it was the right and profitable thing to do.

It was unclear for mainstream operations how such organizations actually worked, and in 1984, researchers began to take a look to find out what makes reliable organizations reliable. The focus of the studies was on organizations that seemed to behave very reliably, which they referred to as high-reliability organizations (HROs), marking the birth of the concept of HROs (Roberts, 2003). One of the first findings was that reliability doesn't necessarily mean safety. The "culture of reliability" is the belief that accidents won't happen if every system participant and component performs reliably. It turns out that very safe systems are not always reliable, and highly reliable systems are not always safe, but the general theory is that increasing reliability should increase safety. In engineering, reliability is the likelihood that a component will satisfy its stated behavioral requirements over time and under certain circumstances. The human is a critical component as well, and human operators are considered unreliable if they do not follow the prescribed procedures. This has been a key metric in the formulation of holistic safety, which is the expected outcome of highly reliable organizations. From this, the current concept of HROs was born.

One more example that makes the case for doing things right when it comes to reinventing an organization into an HRO is British Petroleum's (BP) attempt in the early 2000s. Indeed, the company's executives were right to think that frontline workers needed to be taught mindfulness and be empowered to report warnings of danger. However, this failed dismally, resulting first in the 2005 Texas Refinery accident and, subsequently, the Gulf Oil Spill. Although BP tried to implement the transformation with the right idea, several pieces were missed, leading to the failure. This outcome is consistent with the researchers' findings that for an organization to be successful, it must have all the features of an HRO regardless of the field. Remove one principle, and true reliability will be impossible to achieve. Exxon Mobil's decision to cap the Blackbeard oil well four years before the BP oil spill offers a parallel to this outcome and is considered an important lesson on how leaders need to be able to make decisions based on reality.

Today, the medical field leads the way in deploying HRO principles as medical procedures and processes become more complex and integrated. The demand for HROs will only grow to include other sectors where this concept is still in its infancy. According to Pool (1997), "In a generation or two, the world will likely need thousands of high-reliability organizations running not just nuclear power plants, space flights, and air traffic control, but also chemical plants, electrical grids, computers, and telecommunication networks" among others. The consensus is that the knowledge to transform organizations into HROs is now conclusive, and the challenge lies in the ability of organizations to manage technology and change. Going back to the example of a new facility that was built within an organization where I worked, introducing the technology was the easy part, but managing it reliably at the early stages proved to be difficult and required persistence in identifying the causes of the problems being experienced.

Features of HROs

Even though HROs have fewer than normal accidents despite the associated risk, organizations have to put in the work to develop features that make them better at maintaining their reliability. First, the work has to be done on having the mechanisms in place and also ensuring that the mechanisms are respected. These mechanisms work predominantly because the entire organization works to develop a culture that places emphasis on safety; otherwise, the organization can become a low-reliability organization quickly. This is not just about the outcome but has more to do with how HROs understand the processes that lead to safe outcomes. The understanding is that one small error can lead to a disaster, and if the bases are covered from the grassroots, then no error can be found on the end products or services. The unique features of HROs are that they:

- **Continuously reinvent themselves:** To remain successful, an organization must be able to continuously learn and adapt to new situations based on past lessons. The Navy is a great example to consider. The same facilities are used regardless of whether the operation is a rescue mission or an attack. This is because what already exists is usually more reliable and cheaper to repurpose than a new system altogether. You will notice that aircraft manufacturers have the same approach and are not usually keen on developing a new aircraft from scratch but rather try to use existing models as a base for a new model instead. This is flexibility that is designed to improvise on existing structures. Another example is that of an aircraft carrier, which can utilize its functional units differently depending on the nature of the mission.

- **Have multilateral but coordinated decision-making:** There is no single authority in the decision-making process, although there can be one final authority to sign off on things officially. However, decisions are discussed, and decision-making migrates down to the lowest level consistent with decision implementation. Everyone is allowed to contribute to the decision-making process, and there is a negative impact on reliability when decisions are not checked and validated. Look at the U.S.S. Greenville submarine's crash into a Japanese training fishing boat. The event partly occurred because the commanding officer's decisions to have civilians in the control room and to depart without performing repairs to the video monitor were not questioned by the control technician and the sonar operator, despite this being a requirement detailed in their job descriptions. These and other decisions that breached the regulations led to the collision when the submarine resurfaced (National Transportation Safety Board, n.d.). Similar problems existed in the early years of commercial aviation before

Crew Resource Management.

- **Advocate for teamwork:** Effective teamwork has been the focus of hospitals when they started out by introducing the concepts of HROs into their operations. Most invasive surgeries are a collective effort between different people, and for more complex procedures, professionals from different departments can be required to work together. An error here can have catastrophic consequences, and the early proponents of HROs in the medical field emphasized individual mindfulness for the collaborations to work. This maximizes the synchronization between teams. If you look at the coordination that ATC has with the ground crew, flight crew, and other ATC towers, it is obvious that the key ingredient for flawless flight operations is synchronized teamwork. Everyone knows where everyone is and what they are doing. If there is an anomaly, everyone involved will play their role in a coordinated manner to fix the problem. The same goes for military naval operations. Communication is shared, with status differentials at sea, while allowing people with the right knowledge to make decisions, which are checked. Going back to BP's effort to transform into an HRO, one of the missing links was management's inability to take warnings seriously despite the encouragement for workers to change their mindset when it comes to warnings. Teamwork was absent between the management and the rest of the workforce, meaning the vigilance of the frontline workers did not yield the intended results, making the case that commitment from the top should go beyond policy and procedures.

Managing HROs

To make this commitment work, organizations must have ways to manage the new behaviors. According to Roberts et.al (2005), one reliable model for this purpose was developed by Carolyn Libuser. The model details five management processes: process auditing, implementing reward systems, avoiding quality degradation, command and control, and risk perception. Process auditing requires a system that checks that things are working correctly. This is a performance check designed to find out what is working properly and what is not. If problems are discovered, they need to be addressed. For new systems, testing forms an integral part of the process and must be conducted before anything is certified or given the green light for operation. The Challenger Disaster is also another example of a failed audit system. In this case, the testing that was part of the auditing system showed that the solid rocket booster's O-rings would likely fail, but this was disregarded by both the manufacturer and NASA.

A critical part of the auditing system is following up to ensure that the discovered problem has been addressed and the appropriate procedures have been followed. In the case of the 737 Max, Boeing had the chance to fix the handling characteristics of the aircraft when the prototype was first flown by its chief testing pilot. Instead, the company chose to cover up the seriousness of the problem and quietly introduced the MCAS system as a fix to the problem. While the fix itself worked, two critical follow-ups that would have made the audit work were not done. Boeing never went to the Federal Aviation Authority (FAA) to inform the regulator about what MCAS actually was and the significance of the fix to the end user. After the first accident, "the FAA's prediction following the first crash that flaws in Boeing's system could cause additional crashes in the coming years received no follow-up until the second crash occurred" (Crail & Lupini, 2021). Failure to follow up led to catastrophe and experience shows that the follow-up process needs re-verification to be sure that the data is reliable.

Comparing this with the experience of a new facility discussed in the introduction, a connection can be made between process auditing and preoccupation with failure. After implementing the fix to the pressure vessel, the results had to be closely monitored to ensure that the fix was reliable before new standards to add an internal vessel inspection checklist could be implemented. It is essential that when an audit reveals problems, the findings must be evaluated, classified, and followed with persistent efforts to find the cause of the problem to develop a solution. Building on this are good reward systems. Without the appropriate reward systems, the issues are less likely to be fixed because of the lack of incentive. Rewards are better motivators compared to punishment. Even at the prospect of being caught by the regulators, Boeing's executives chose to participate in the cover-up because there was a financial incentive to do this. Covering the real impact of MCAS meant the planes sold like hotcakes, and the reward for hiding the problems seemingly outweighed the potential punishment if the malpractice was caught.

Another management tool is a framework for upholding quality standards. This involves staying clear of practices, designs, and processes that reduce quality. Standards such as the American Society of Mechanical Engineers (ASME) exist as a benchmark for acceptable standards for quite a number of things. Again, Boeing failed at this by designing a system that relied on a single angle of attack (AoA) sensor, even at the objection of some engineers who were part of the program, according to the internal documents. Upholding quality standards improves another management tool, which is risk perception. This is divided into two parts, namely risk awareness and risk acknowledgment. Risk can be loosely defined as "a probability of occurrence and consequences of some adverse event" and is regarded as a complex phenomenon (Krasnopevtseva et al., 2019). The final piece of the model is command and control, which covers five processes. Its role is to tie everything together, emphasizing the role of specific people to manage risk and perceive events within the organization's big picture that integrates error-avoiding processes. An illustration of this is a Venn diagram, which shows the entire story, but separate sets make contributions to the full story.

Overall, the processes must

- facilitate deference to expertise.

- build redundancy into teams and hardware.

- develop senior managers and executives

who can focus on the bigger picture.

- implement formal rules and procedures.

- include training for teams.

Principles of HROs

Libuser's management model lays the necessary foundation for organizations to begin looking at how they can implement the five principles of HROs. The first principle is preoccupation with failure. HROs are obsessed with finding the cause of a deviation from normal results, failure, or problem, no matter how small. Every malfunction is closely examined because it can be a sign of a bigger problem. Secondly, when problems are found, there is a reluctance to simplify the cause of the problem. This is the second principle. HROs are reluctant to accept simplification because this gives room for critical data or information to be left out, which might be useful to solve or diagnose a problem.

High Reliability Organizations:
Building Blocks for Success

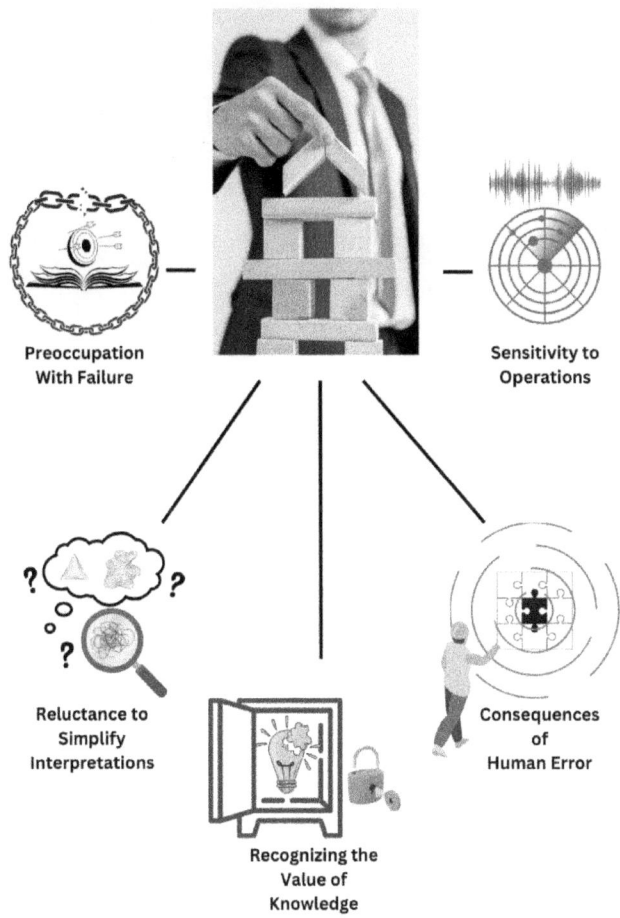

Preoccupation
With Failure

Sensitivity to
Operations

Reluctance to
Simplify
Interpretations

Consequences
of
Human Error

Recognizing the
Value of
Knowledge

The third principle is that HROs are sensitive to operations. This means that they closely monitor and pay attention to what is happening as it happens. There is a bird's eye view of the operations, and managers should pay attention to discrete components and the system as a whole. Continuous assessment is performed to evaluate the outcomes against the organization's goals. HROs do not presume that the observed behavior or outcome should be the same as what was anticipated, planned, or hoped for. In this regard, HROs view the outcomes as practical experiences from which the organization's operations can be further improved in the present. In addition to this, HROs commit to resilience, which is the fourth principle. Organizations constantly subject their systems to extreme stress. HROs are aware that they must constantly adapt to changing conditions. Three essential traits make up resilience. If your company can absorb pressure and keep operating in challenging circumstances or "bounce back" from setbacks and learn from them, then it is resilient.

Finally, HROs exhibit deference to expertise. This means that importance is placed on who can solve the problem we have instead of who is qualified to solve the problem. Mechanisms to identify knowledgeable people must be available. The focus is hands-on knowledge and expertise for decision-making rather than formal authority to deal with unexpected occurrences that test resilience. People with practical hands-on knowledge must be given liberty to report to higher authority and influence desired outcomes. This goes beyond just knowing and adds credibility, trust, and attentiveness. People in HRO organizations recognize and share what they know, even if no one wants to hear it.

These principles will be looked at individually later on, but for now, let's shift our focus to cases of accidents that have dominated the subject of high-reliability organizations. We have already discussed the mistakes Boeing and BP made, but there are other disasters to learn from, notably the *Bhopal* chemical disaster, the *Challenger* disaster, and the *Three Mile Island* nuclear incident. The discussion will start with the *normal accident theory*, which many organizations still rely on to develop strategies to deal with accidents, and how the theory compares with the thinking behind HROs. There are similarities between the two as well as differences, which, in the end, make HROs superior to organizations that approach incidents from the perspective of normal accident theory.

Chapter 2

HRO Case Studies

Normal Accident Theory (NAT) and HROs are both valuable concepts that help organizations deal with safety and risk management in complex systems. A major overlap between the two approaches is the simplification of the cause of accidents and the solutions to reduce the chances of accidents occurring. Let's look at NAT first. The theory "recognizes the difficulty of dealing with uncertainty but underestimates and oversimplifies the potential ways to cope with uncertainty" (Hviid, 2021). HRO theory, however, offers more suggestions to limit risk, but the challenge is that if unrefined, the solutions are inapplicable to most complex systems and result in broad application of the challenges. There is a risk that organizations may become complacent or overconfident in their safety practices if they believe that accidents can always be prevented.

This is where most managers struggle, particularly when there is a lack of experience in dealing with problems within the same company or field of operations.

Going to the differences, much of it lies in the two mindsets that the two approaches encourage. Normal Accident Theory (NAT) considers major accidents as inevitable in high-risk operations. The theory focuses on methods to reduce risk but limits the role of proactive action from organizations when it comes to implementing safety measures because, according to the theory, accidents cannot be prevented in complex systems. The reasoning behind this is that accidents happen because of inherent system characteristics that make it difficult to anticipate, and as a result, possible accidents cannot be fully conceived, and outcomes cannot be controlled. This is not to say that NAT is not useful. One of the advantages of using this theory is that organizations can realize the limits of safety management, so only realistic measures can be implemented to mitigate risk. For an organization that is focused on balancing safety and profitability, this can help develop ways of managing risk with the knowledge that nothing is 100% safe.

Overall, the theories of normal accidents and high-reliability organizations present different viewpoints on risk in complex systems. While the NAT holds that accidents are unavoidable, HRO theory presents a set of guidelines that can assist organizations in preventing errors and enhancing safety. The bottom line is that HRO represents a social response to ambiguity, complexity, and threat from both a behavioral and physical perspective, whereas NAT describes the results of interactions between humans and machines, viewing this relationship as a source of threat to safety and reliability. HRO administers a solution that is successful, while NAT diagnoses the problem or rather explains why things happen before seeking to limit the risks associated. The solution-orientated approach of HRO makes it more desirable for organizations that seek to improve reliability. To understand this further, let's take a deeper look at three case studies that are pertinent to our discussion.

Three Mile Island Nuclear Incident

Reports indicate that around 2 million residents of the surrounding area were put in danger after being exposed to tiny doses of radiation when the nuclear rods of the Three Mile Island nuclear plant overheated and melted (United States Nuclear Regulatory Commission, 2022). Fortunately, the radiation levels were insufficient to cause any potential health side effects, but the incident is considered the most serious nuclear accident involving a nuclear power plant in the US. It all started when a valve in the secondary cooling circuit was stuck in the open position. Due to this, the cooling water escaped from the system, resulting in the loss of coolant and the subsequent overheating of the fuel rods. The operators did not immediately realize what was going on partly because of the confusing and contradicting system error messages leading to delayed corrective action. More gravely, the operators shut down the emergency water cooling system for the reactor, thinking that the water levels were sufficient due to the high system pressure. It is beneficial to look at the sequence of events within the Three Mile Plant itself.

- The accident was initiated by a shutdown of the pumps feeding water to the secondary loop. One second later, the alarm sounded and was disregarded by operators because the increase in temperature and pressure was considered normal.

- After three seconds, the Pilot-operated Relief Valve (PORV) opens as designed to let off excess steam. Back-up water pumps also turn on as designed. By then, the operators had already missed that water was not flowing through the pump.

- Two minutes in, the emergency water injection is turned on automatically. This is part of the design intended to ensure that water in the core remains at a safe level. However, there had been past events where the system turned on automatically without a coolant leak, so the operators turned the system off. Forty-five minutes into the event, the operators still had not realized that they were losing coolant.

- Two hours and twenty minutes in, the operator from the next shift arrived, realized what was happening, and closed the PORV valve.

- Around sixteen hours after the situation began, a number of events occurred, and the core melted with hydrogen present in the primary loop. Radiation had already leaked before the core's temperature was finally brought under control.

The main reason behind the operators' inability to correctly identify the problem was a lack of instruments to signal that the valve was not in the closed position. All they had was an indication that the signal to "close" had been sent. A series of other built-in responses occurred, but the most important action identified during the investigation was that the operators responded by "reducing the flow of replacement water" (World Nuclear Association, 2022). This further starved the core of the critical coolant required. The actions taken were informed by training as the operators were trained to rely on the pressurizer water level as the sole indicator of cooling water in the system. Steam formed in the cooling system, and this led to severe vibrations in the cooling pumps. In order to reduce damage to the pumps, the pumps were shut down, with forced cooling being the final action in a bid to cool the system. However, the primary cause of the problem was missed. Considering the sequence of events from the perspective of the reluctance to simplify, it is clear that any anomaly can significantly affect reliability, no matter how small the relationship between the error and the outcome can appear to be. This is what the principle of "reluctance to simplify" attempts to counter.

In hindsight, it can also be said that the organization failed to reinvent itself because lessons from the past were not learned. Pigford (1981) noted that "earlier experience from other reactors and analyses dating back to 1972 should have alerted the industry, the regulatory agency, and the operators and avoided the accident." The exact problem with the PORV had previously occurred 11 times, and the same situation that Three Mile experienced had occurred at the Davis-Besse Nuclear Power Station over a year before the incident. A knowledge of these issues could have been factored into the facility's standard operating procedures. Instead, the actions taken worsened the situation, resulting in more coolant being lost, further melting, and the release of the radioactive material.

The Accident in the Context of NAT and HRO

The disaster can be explained in the context of normal accident theory because the event was a combination of multiple failures in a complex system. The NAT was actually developed based on the incident, and we know why the accident happened from this perspective. Specifically, the reasons are that a complex system failed, and the human interaction with the system compounded the errors in unexpected ways. The accident can be considered an outcome of systematic failure due to the complexity of the system. In this context, the accident was not a result of individual human error but rather a systemic failure that was inherent to the complexity of the system.

Similarly, the accident can be explained from the perspective of HRO. The nuclear facility had safety operational procedures, of course; however, the response to the failure was not good enough, and poor coordination, whether at the frontline or within the company as a whole, ultimately led to the operators failing to manage the crisis in real time. Among the operators and management, there was a lack of teamwork and situational awareness that could have led to a proper diagnosis of the problem. From the same accident, we can see that NAT stresses the complexity of the causes, while HRO explains accidents from the perspective of organizational and cultural factors with regard to the outcome. Overall, reliability failed at the frontlines.

The Challenger Disaster

The next disaster worth looking at is the Challenger Disaster, which occurred on January 28, 1986, when the space shuttle, Challenger, broke apart just 73 seconds into its flight. All crew members on board were killed, and the disaster was attributed to the breach of an O-ring seal in one of the solid rocket boosters (SRB), allowing the hot gasses to escape and damage the shuttle's external fuel tank, leading to its explosion. Quite a number of things contributed to the disaster. NASA made a series of mistakes due to public pressure and needed to launch the shuttle on time. This led to several decisions that compromised the safety of the shuttle, especially the decision to disregard warnings from engineers about the deficiencies, as well as the test data that showed the O-ring seals would fail at cold temperatures. In a bold statement, one of the engineers on the project recalled that "we all knew if the seals failed, the shuttle would blow up" (Berkes, 2016). Besides the simulation data, the engineers pointed to the fact that previous cold temperature launches resulted in a noticeable compromise to the O-ring's integrity. Despite these warnings, the managers at NASA went ahead with the launch, disregarding the risks to the crew's safety. The engineers who had raised concerns were overruled to meet the agency's launch schedule. NASA's culture of hierarchy and top-down decision-making made it difficult for lower-level employees to challenge authority and speak up about safety concerns.

In addition to this, NASA was complacent and practiced normalization of deviance, where risks and anomalies were often overlooked or dismissed as insignificant. Normalization of deviance is at odds with the principles of HRO and is defined as "the process by which deviance from correct or proper behavior becomes normalized in a corporate culture" (VanderMey, 2020). Whenever this occurs, safety standards are compromised, and risky behavior becomes more acceptable. The tragedy is that unlike the Three Mile Nuclear incident, in which there was an effort to follow the rules, obvious problems were ignored, leading to the highest authorities signing off on the launch with malfunctioning equipment with components that had clearly failed simulations.

The Challenger and HRO

The case of the Challenger provides clear evidence of violations of the principles of HROs. Consider preoccupation with failure, for instance, which was absent in the case of the Challenger disaster. Not only was the data available, but previous launches clearly indicated that the O-rings were susceptible to malfunction in cold temperatures, and the decision to ignore this is evidence that the operation did not preoccupy itself with failure. The failure of NASA to heed the calls also shows that there was no sensitivity to operations, which is rooted in the idea that operations do not assume that the continuous outcomes will be the same as planned. Finally, NASA did not demonstrate commitment to resilience because there was a single point of failure. NASA did not have adequate contingency plans, if any, in place to address the failure of the O-rings, and when this failed, the whole operation failed. Overall, even though the team on the ground displayed the characteristics of a high-performing team, the lack of accountability on the leadership meant that their knowledge and experience could not prevent the disaster. In this case, reliability failed at the very top.

Bhopal Chemical Leak

The Bhopal Chemical Leak, considered to be the world's worst industrial disaster, occurred in India in December of 1984 after methyl isocyanate gas was released from the pesticide manufacturing plant, in which just over 3,000 people were killed. Other estimates put these figures to more than 20,000 killed over the course of time, and around half a million people were exposed to the cloud of toxic fumes (Curtis & Gill, 2022). The disaster is another example of an accident in a complex environment primarily as a result of design flaws in the plant, poor safety measures, and operational errors. The sequence of events started when water entered the storage tank containing the isocyanate gas, resulting in a chemical reaction. The systems designed to prevent the release of the gas into the atmosphere failed dismally, and compounding this was the absence of emergency response procedures in the event of a total systems failure. There had been previous leaks in the plant, which could have prevented the disaster, but no corrective action had been taken in another example of failure to learn from past mistakes. What is more tragic is that the operator, Union Carbide Corporation, made an attempt to distance itself from the disaster and presented several arguments, including sabotage, a clear departure from the principle of accountability that guides the operations of HROs.

First, analyzing the disaster from the concept of NAT, it could be said that the disaster was inevitable due to the complexity of the operation and the unpredictability that comes with it. Looking at the leaks before the disaster and the actions of the operator gives an opportunity to understand the effectiveness of HRO principles in mitigating disasters because, in reality, the accident occurred primarily from the culture of the operator rather than the complexity of the system itself. The operator failed to uphold the principles of HROs that focus on recognizing that while accidents do happen, it is the responsibility of the organization to take proactive steps to build systems and processes that are resilient and adaptable to dangerous situations. In this regard, preoccupation with failure was absent, the plant lacked redundancy, and operations did not consider the risks, particularly when it came to keeping large quantities of reactive chemicals.

This lack of accountability is evident even from the initial stages of plant operation. The entire plant was a blueprint of Union Carbide's facilities across the world, yet corners were cut during the construction of the plant. For instance, the equipment containing methyl isocyanate was made of corrosion-prone carbon steel instead of stainless steel, according to the plant specifications, while the seals were made of ceramic instead of metal.

One more feature of HROs is the recognition that small errors or anomalies can lead to big failures, according to the principle of sensitivity to operations. No action was taken after the first small leak that killed one worker and the following leak, which led to the hospitalization of dozens more, regardless of the complaints from frontline workers that the operations were unsafe. There were multiple warnings before the disaster, which should have compelled corrective action to be taken, and the disaster could have been avoided. Lastly, there was no commitment to resilience because no systems were in place to respond to an emergency. HROs understand that failures will occur, and they prepare for them by building resilient systems and processes.

United Airlines Flight 232

This incident is an example of how operations that adopt all HRO principles can control outcomes when one part of a complex system fails or makes a mistake. United Airlines Flight 232 was a scheduled flight that suffered a catastrophic failure when the engine-mounted tail failed in mid-air. This led to a complete loss of control at high altitudes after the loss of hydraulic fluid. The only available method to control the aircraft was the throttle levers for the two remaining engines using asymmetric thrust for directional control, which was not yet an established procedure at the time. Despite the loss of human life, with 111 passenger lives lost and 185 survivors, the aircraft crash landed due to the crew's adherence to the principles of HROs (Green, 2022). Preoccupation with failure was built into the operations and crew's culture, first reflected in the training and the ability to diagnose what the problem actually was and recognize the limitations of the operation following the failure. Despite the total loss of hydraulics being previously inconceivable, the crew was quick to notice that they would need to work with all possible solutions because there was no simple explanation for the problem. The other action taken by the commanding captain was to call in another captain in the cabin who was off duty but an experienced training captain, a clear demonstration of the difference in expertise. In addition, the crew contacted the maintenance control and aircraft control to get additional assistance for this unique disaster. All hands were on deck, and every idea was heard and discussed. Throughout the chaos, the crew remained aware of the other factors important to the flight, such as weather, and managed to keep the cabin crew informed while maintaining altitude using unorthodox means. Finally, the crew remained committed to finding a solution and worked together to use all available resources to save the passengers and the aircraft, demonstrating commitment to resilience. According to the Federal Aviation Administration (2022), the crew discussed whether to extend the landing gear or not, exploring a number of scenarios and how this action would affect the stability they had managed to achieve. Following the crash, subsequent simulations during the investigation failed to recreate the actions of the crew, and had it not been for the crew's ability to implement principles of HRO in their crew resource management, the outcome would have been more tragic.

The Three Miles Incident, the Challenger disaster, and the Bhopal Chemical disaster are examples of the outcome when one or more HRO principles are broken. The Three Mile nuclear incident shows the importance of organizational culture when it comes to problem-solving, especially when there is incomplete information about the nature of the problem. The other two cases illustrate what can happen when there is no accountability at the top. For organizations to be truly HROs, all the pieces of the puzzle should be in place, and when people at the top are accountable, high-performing teams are able to solve problems more effectively and coordinate their behavior when confronted with unique problems. The next chapter explores how to create interlocking organizational reliability with an emphasis on developing high-reliability teams, as illustrated in the example of United Airlines Flight 232, and how the Challenger disaster could have been avoided.

Chapter 3

Creating Interlocking Organizational Reliability

Whatever we plant in our subconscious mind and nourish with repetition and emotion will one day become a reality. –Earl Nightingale

A culture of "collective mindfulness" is at the heart of HROs, where all employees pay attention to the smallest issues and report seemingly minor issues or unsafe situations before they become serious risks to the company and while they are still relatively simple to address. To promote group mindfulness and behavior, organizations need strong leadership commitment, comprehensive process improvement, and a safety-oriented culture. As decision-makers for organizational strategy, leaders set the stage for the organization to be a high-reliability organization. Another example worth considering is the case of Samsung when one of its models, the Galaxy Note 7, was launched. Similar to how Boeing had responded to Airbus's A320 Neo with the Max, the executives at Samsung decided to outsmart Apple and launch their smartphone first. A few weeks after the launch of the devices, the batteries started to catch fire, leading to recalls and billions in revenue lost (Tsukayama, 2018). This rush led to design flaws, with the batteries being ignored, putting the company's reputation at risk. The next section looks at the responsibilities that executives and managers have for their organizations to become HRO organizations. This will be broken into the responsibilities of the executives responsible for decision-making and mid-level managers who are responsible for the daily operations of the organization.

Developing an HRO Mindset for Executives

Risk Acknowledgement

To open the possibilities of zero harm requires leaders in organizations to acknowledge that their environment, services, or products are high risk to the public. At the core of this is the ability to admit to mistakes when they have been made. This puts things into perspective and guides the decisions that are made across all business operations. You will notice that once this responsibility has been accepted at the highest level, certain questions begin to form part of the decision-making process, and among them are questions that seek to discover where problems are likely to arise from and potential sources of failure so that the concerns can be improved.

Driving Data

A common challenge that leaders face is that they need to meet the expectations of investors and stakeholders, which adds to the pressure when it comes to making decisions that could eat into the profitability of the organization. The blame for the Challenger disaster can be largely placed on the management's lack of willingness to look at the data because of the launch schedule. This is where scenario planning and the "what-if" questions come into play. Looking at the data helps with seeing beyond the curve. At the slightest hint that there is a possibility that something is off, the leadership has a responsibility to look at all angles with the information available. It is rare for data to paint a wrong picture because it is evidence of past behaviors or a prediction of how things can turn out. The same thing happened with Boeing. The initial test flight of the 737 Max showed that something was terribly wrong with the plane's handling, yet this data was ignored because profits needed to be achieved at all costs, despite what the data was showing. Be willing to look at the data that lower-level employees are presenting and show diligence in making sure that all concerns have been addressed. HROs continuously learn more about the elements that lead to errors or incidents and take preventative action by reviewing historical data. This supports decision-making and knowledge management.

Another dimension when it comes to data in today's world is "Big Data." If your organization is large or, more precisely, can gather a lot of data throughout the production or service delivery cycle, then data science must be seriously considered to find patterns and trends for better decision-making and recommendations. You will see that a clearer picture can be painted when trying to solve a problem, and sometimes, the culture of just collecting data and analyzing it can uncover problems not yet known. This can facilitate predictive maintenance, which in turn is useful to forecast when equipment is likely to fail to make concepts like just-in-time maintenance more effective. Additionally, the cost of operations will be reduced as a result of minimum equipment-related downtime for operations. An example of an organization that uses predictive maintenance effectively is General Electric, which is one of the leading aircraft engine manufacturers. Regardless of the scale of operations, integrating predictive maintenance for the purpose of high reliability can be achieved by collecting data for analysis, condition monitoring, and deployment of predictive algorithms to find errors or identify patterns (*Predictive Maintenance*, n.d.).

Contextualizing Errors and Mistakes

Having a mindset that looks at mistakes objectively will help with decision-making to correct the errors. High-reliability drivers have a growth mindset that admits to mistakes with the goal of learning from them. As a leader, you are better positioned to ask questions such as: What or how is the situation now, what must be done to make our products safe, and what must we change or put in place to prevent this from happening again, leading to continuous improvement. Such questions bring the organization closer to high reliability with each lesson learned. One thing I have learned through experience is that the leader doesn't need to have all the answers but must be willing to listen to all the solutions to a problem. Once all the possible solutions are on the table, these can be optimized for a balanced solution that is in line with the organization's goals.

Overall, executives can set their organizations on the right path by:

- **Adopting model-based approaches:** Model-based approaches shift focus to proactivity rather than reactivity. The two examples of Boeing and Samsung are cases of reactive leadership. Reactivity to either competition or an incident puts the organization on a back foot, and for incidents when there are no redundancies in place, half-baked solutions can be introduced to make a bad situation worse. The principles discussed later on in the book are designed to keep the organization proactive, even when confronted with an unfamiliar situation. Being reactive does not matter much if action is taken after a serious event that could have been prevented through proactive action. There are several forecasting techniques and models that executives and leaders can utilize, and most of them rely on risk identification, risk anticipation, and enhanced communication. Simulations are a great proactive tool that leaders should champion because different scenarios can be modeled and communications built around outcomes. The next logical step would be continuous improvement based on the data and assessments, whether process or performance-oriented.

- **Taking responsibility for system issues:** Punishing and blaming employees rather than looking at the entire system threatens reliability. Mistakes do happen, and even experienced professionals make mistakes. Placing blame increases the chances of mistakes being swept under the rug in an effort to avoid punishment. Focus on developing open and safe incident reporting systems where everyone can speak up without fear of reprisal. When mistakes are brought to the leadership's attention, there must be a process to diagnose errors, and models such as the Just Culture Decision Tree are useful to get to the root of the problem. The tool has three branches, which are focused on human error, system error, and predictable error. The Three Mile Nuclear Incident is a clear example of a system failure, and while the operators shared the blame, it is the system that should have been designed with fail-safe mechanisms to make it impossible for operator error to occur. Approaching errors from the perspective of system errors is an attempt to find out if this error had been predicted before or if this possibility was completely missed. You will then need to diagnose why the predictions missed the errors, and if there were no predictions at all, find out why. There could be many reasons for this. For instance, it could be that the needed resources were not channeled to simulations or error forecasting, and this will need to be addressed within the system, whether through the risk department or R&D. You will still need to consider human error, but be sure to objectively look at whether the human error is a result of reckless behavior warranting disciplinary action or a simple mistake, which will also need to be corrected through training. External factors can also lead to unpredictable errors, especially in risky operations where knowledge is limited or still evolving. Remaining on top of the situation requires paying attention to the details and focusing on the appropriate issues at the right time. Other techniques and models that can be used when diagnosing system issues include the five whys technique, which features probing questions designed to get to the root of the problem.

Developing an HRO Mindset for Managers

Managers act as the implementers of the executives' efforts to develop an HRO culture and are greatly involved in operationalizing HROs. Needed is a mindset fertile for overcoming the barriers that most managers face when they try to transform their organizations. You need to think differently to effect culture change, and this starts with accountability, which must be interlocked into daily operations. Floor managers can have their own departmental policies, which can be as simple as the open-door policy. Integrate reliability into the team through education, coaching, and training. While the operationalization of HROs is a top-down approach, your role as the manager is to quarterback the transformation, meaning you become the link between the executives and the frontline employees.

- **Make effective improvements:** Another potential source of unreliability is when changes are made in an effort to improve how things are done. Process improvements need to consider the downstream implications and remain within the organization's best practices and policies, executing organizational processes and ensuring practices adhere to the company vision. One example is a hospital setting in which a process improvement was made to reduce mislabeled blood specimens by implementing a "final check," which required staff to read out the last three digits of the medical record number on the label and compare this with the number on the patient's wrist. Effective process improvements are not radical but rather add a simple step in a process that already exists.

- **Take advantage of problem-solving:** Last but not least, managers must be able to foster a culture of creative problem-solving. To do this successfully, they must encourage creative thinking and also allow those under them to fail. Like innovation, failure needs to be managed by reducing risk and negligent behavior. Solutions to problems must be well thought out, and even if the solutions fail, these failures help to develop a culture of continuous learning. In addition to learning from past mistakes, this should also include learning professionally to keep up with changes or news happening in the industry. The Three Mile Island disaster could have been avoided if the organization had knowledge of the prior incident with the valves. It is essential to find a time when teams are allowed to reflect and discuss things happening elsewhere. All this is crucial to individual and collective problem-solving. A balance is required, however, because solutions need to be filtered. This builds on the principle of deference to expertise, but a balance is needed when solving problems. Managers need to set the right conditions, and employees must remain accountable for what they do. The atmosphere that is created ultimately allows others to speak up.

In the next chapter, I will share an example of how a new employee questioned the purpose of the "emergency exit" that had been normalized as an ordinary entrance. Employees who are preoccupied with failure can easily speak up if the environment is right. Such an environment also makes it possible for deference to expertise to be tolerated. An organization might have a policy that promotes deference to expertise on paper, but if the culture is not practiced in daily operations, then it will be difficult for the ordinary employee to speak without authority despite having the skills to fix the problem.

The above makes it clear that transforming an organization into an HRO starts from the top, but zero harm is achievable when the entire organization is working from the same playbook. Senior and mid-level managers are responsible for creating an environment that enables the employees on the floor to develop an HRO-oriented mindset. This mindset is the foundation to operationalize a high-reliability organization that is built around high-reliability teams.

Chapter 4

Operationalizing a High-Reliability Organization

A great leader takes people where they don't necessarily want to go, but ought to be.
–Rosalynn Carter

Once the culture of reliability has been fostered at the top, an organization begins to think about how to operationalize high-reliability concepts at the bottom. Naturally, this should filter through to the entire organization, but the challenge is that it can be difficult to measure the extent to which the organizational culture has changed because teams and individuals develop this mindset at different levels. Nowadays, organizations have anonymous feedback and surveys that are sent out to find out from employees how they feel about the organization in general. On the floor, you can easily notice that the culture is changing based on the behavior, feedback, or input from the frontline employees. This brings us to the conversation with the new hire mentioned in the previous chapter. For a long time, the organization's premises had a door that had been marked as a fire exit and equipped with a buzzer when opened. Over time, employees began to use the door as a normal entrance, defeating the purpose of the door. Although this had been normalized, the fact that a new hire was comfortable with speaking up and challenging a practice that had been going on for years is evidence of an HRO culture. The other side of the coin is being able to implement the appropriate changes. In this case, the warning signs were removed, and the door became a normal entrance officially.

Operationalization is a method or set of processes defining how a phenomenon is measured. Consider a car, for example. Each person has an opinion of what they consider a reliable car, but you can easily find one or two common themes when a group of people is asked what they consider to be a reliable car. Often, this will fall into a car that does not usually break down, even when the conditions of operation are not suitable for the vehicle's use. Others consider a car to be reliable when it does what it is supposed to do with a reasonable frequency of servicing and no major failures of critical components. Car makers think about this when they are designing the vehicle. For instance, German car makers like Volkswagen and BMW think about vehicles using the lens of "how do we want consumers to use our vehicles?" while Japanese car makers like Toyota think about the cars from the perspective of "how will the consumer use the product." In the end, vehicles from German automakers need the owner to be more involved and pay attention to maintenance, and negligence can lead to a vehicle that breaks down frequently. The different design philosophies and subsequent differences in how the manufacturers approach reliability lead to Japanese vehicles being considered more reliable than German vehicles from the end user's perspective (Grigelevičius, 2022). Other examples of phenomena that are difficult to quantify are social phenomena such as personal space, and for an organization that seeks to be an HRO, the task is to quantify and define what reliability is from the perspective of all stakeholders. You can use practical observations to understand and explain reliability to the employees.

Cultural Analysis

Once you have defined reliability and formed a baseline of the needed change in culture, the next step is to discover what employees think about reliability within the organization or its products. For this initial step of operationalizing, it is essential to find out how your organization is doing right now instead of focusing on metrics such as event rates, which are poor measures of actual exposure. This is an auditing process. Going back to the example of a new hire's inquiry on the use of an emergency exit as a normal entrance, there had not been a single instance of an emergency that created confusion on its use, meaning the event rate was zero in this case. However, this did not translate to zero exposure. It is likely that there would be problems with executing an evacuation if a fire had broken out. Once you understand the current culture of the employees, the findings can be used as a baseline to effect cultural change, and this change must be clear on the goals of reliability. Resilience should be the direct outcome of cultural change, and the concept of resilience engineering is embedded in how HROs behave. In essence, resilience engineering focuses on managing failures through training that builds adaptable individuals in complex settings. We will meet this concept later on, but consequently, it becomes essential to find out what employees think to identify gaps that can be addressed through corrective training and education. Furthermore, it is imperative that reliability is quantified as much as possible so that there is a measurable goal against the organization's definition of reliability.

Cultural Change Barriers

People don't like change and are usually resistant, especially when it appears to be coming from an external source. Individual resistance to change is the main barrier managers will face when they try to implement HRO principles at the team level. Two possible reasons can explain this. Number one, change brings uncertainty, and employees can be unwilling to change if they feel that their jobs are on the line. Sometimes, building reliability might mean increasing automation, which, if not explained, can lead to uncooperative teams. The second reason is the presentation. It should be made clear that it is not their current beliefs at a personal level that is the target, and before the change in culture is enforced, employees must be included in developing the new culture. Managers have an easier job at effecting culture change if the objectives are clear and the process inclusive. A path to bridging the gap between the current and desired culture should also be discussed, and when employees know that they will be trained, this tends to encourage participation. Multicultural settings make the barriers more difficult to overcome, and it is essential for managers to take this into account.

The message surrounding the expectations must also be consistent, and this is where exemplary leadership comes into play. It is important that managers lead from the front. Imagine that you implement a requirement for employees to be at work 10 minutes earlier for a daily debrief into the operations, but you, as the manager, do not make this change. This can invite doubt into the objectives, and employees are reluctant to change if leaders act one way but speak another. The first weeks are crucial to reinforce culture change. The message of cultural transformation must be continually reaffirmed, and leaders must set an example of the desired behaviors. Finally, directions must be clear for employees to know what the expectations are, and there should be room for compromise because it is not always the case where the new requirements are acceptable. If you find yourself facing resistance from the majority of the workforce, then you will need to work out a win-win solution that meets the organization's goals in the best possible way.

Technical Evaluation

Cultural assessments are effective at forecasting and setting reliability goals based on how the employees are currently approaching things. Technical assessments look at the system issues and focus on exposing where the system and processes are vulnerable to risk. The human-system interaction is also considered because processes need the operator's input and, at times, require the operator to interpret what the system is providing as feedback, particularly during abnormal functions. For this, you will need historical data, and if there are planned changes, this data is useful to forecast how the system will behave when changes are implemented.

Historical Focus vs. Future Focus on Reliability

Future-focused operationalization approaches are more reliable compared to historical approaches for several reasons. Organizations that use a historical approach to develop HRO practices only consider high-frequency events that have lagging metrics where only incidents are reported. On the contrary, future-focused approaches report near misses and utilize leading and in-process metrics, including high-consequence events, despite their frequency of occurrence. Another difference lies in the causal factors. In future-oriented approaches, the focus is on organizational and management systems, while only technical and operations factors are important to organizations that take a historical approach. This results in two different philosophies where one always considers the past to predict the future while the other assumes that the worst is possible even if the chance is remote.

Developing High-Reliability Teams

Floor managers, in particular, must make sure that employees understand what reliable teams do. This starts with selecting the right people for the job who are committed to both professional and personal improvement. Managers will need to be process-driven and be able to create a structure that is clear and easy to follow. The processes must be aligned with each team's area of expertise, and where there are shared responsibilities, it must be clear what needs to be done and to whom things should be reported. The AIER model is important to describe how reliable teams should behave after cultural changes and technical improvements have been made. AIER is an acronym for anticipation, inquiry, execution, and resilience. The model is broken down as follows:

- **Anticipation:** When teams have reliable anticipation skills and systems, they become sensitive to weak signals that indicate exposure to risk. For anticipation to be optimized, teams pay attention to deviations and small errors and record this information for analysis. Something such as an abnormal sound from a turbine can be a sign of misalignment, for instance, even if the instruments that measure vibrations do not immediately detect an anomaly. This requires the teams to be vibrant and skilled to know the difference between what is normal and what is not. Safe operating limits must be narrow because wide operating limits introduce chances of something failing. You will notice that organizations with good HRO practices have stricter standards compared to the governing body, and when this is detected, subsequent investigations to understand the reasons are immediately initiated. If the process gets outside its normal operating range, that's an early indication that it didn't function as designed. In order to refine the anticipation skills of your team, it is essential to encourage reporting and reinforce acting on the data. Leaders must be aware of and embrace the fact that there will be a lot of unimportant information, but it is still vital to sort through it to make sure that important information is not overlooked. Even when the examination of these indications does not reveal a major risk, leaders who clearly value the search for early warnings and support this behavior help teams become better at anticipation.

- **Inquiry:** Teams that are inquisitive are better protected from cognitive biases, leading to effective risk management. The main activities are analyzing, understanding, and planning with the objective of risk reduction. Biases can result in flawed decision-making, and it is imperative to remove all forms of bias when looking at factors that affect an organization's reliability. Cognitive bias is a significant factor that can impede the effectiveness of safety management efforts. This refers to the tendency we all have to rely on intuitive thinking to process information efficiently, leading to poor decisions. Snyder (2021) details an example where a crew of maintenance workers responding to the sound of leaking gas from pipelines in a trench assumed that the gas was nitrogen based on the previous leak. In this case, the leak was hydrogen, and when the trench cover was lifted, a spark ignited the hydrogen, and several people were killed. If the work crew had been inquisitive and utilized the four-gas combustible gas indicator instead of making an assumption, the bias would have been eliminated.

The other challenge with cognitive bias is that it can lead to people quickly accepting what is already known. For example, the tendency to go along with a group's predominant opinion can worsen the situation. Biases that can lead to poor decisions include confirmation bias, normalcy bias, availability bias, status quo bias, groupthink, and risk seeking/risk aversion. Culture and leadership are critical to guard against the negative effects of cognitive bias. There are specific leadership behaviors, such as encouraging the voicing of dissenting opinions, that promote a culture that produces more accurate decisions. There are also specific skills involved in asking the right questions in the right way to get the right data. Leaders must promote and measure the use of these leadership skills and behaviors to prevent biases from undermining the effectiveness of safety management efforts. By doing so, organizations can ensure that their safety management efforts are more robust and effective in protecting their teams and assets.

- **Execution:** It's all about execution, and

if this part fails, there is no reliability to talk about because poor execution renders reliability and safety processes useless. For execution to be effective, managers should have the tools to monitor processes and be able to intervene when teams are deviating from the goals of standard operating procedures. Reinforce good behavior and verify that a process is being executed correctly by both the operator and the system. Reinforcement involves providing feedback that recognizes good performance and emphasizes the importance and priority of catastrophic event prevention activities. Effective reinforcement is based on effective monitoring, which provides leaders with specific data to base their feedback on. The feedback must be clear and detailed as much as possible for teams to know where their strengths lie. Vague and ineffective feedback such as "good job" must be avoided at all costs because they offer no reinforcement or expose areas of improvement. For the most part, this involves getting information on a team's performance and progress regularly toward the desired objective and how this is being achieved. This should not be confused with micromanaging teams but rather an assurance that there is sufficient information to recognize good performance and provide support where it is required. Closely related to monitoring is verification. Its objective is to check activities and programs instead of performance, and where auditing finds areas of improvement, managers must make sure that the concerns are addressed in a timely manner.

- **Resilience:** For organizational resilience, the key metric is agility, which is a measure of the organization's ability to react to risk. Highly reliable teams are able to do this in real time in order to prevent small errors from growing into big problems and be able to learn from the experience. If you are a racing sports fan, you can easily see this when a team encounters a big problem during practice or qualifying hours before the main race. They work until the last moment to find out what the problem is and get their racing cars ready for the race. This was the case for the Red Bull Racing Formula One team when their driver crashed during a practice under wet conditions 30 minutes before the actual race (Clayton, 2021). The team was able to fix the suspension and bring the car back onto the track in time for the race. This is an example of agility, and when it comes to HROs, strong resilience is the key to preventing small process disruptions from developing into major incidents. For an organization to develop this resilience, teams must have the knowledge to find out what is going on and fix it, be willing to commit, and have a mindset that is open to continuous learning. HROs should create a knowledge-based organization where employees are trained to make decisions based on their knowledge and the information at hand instead of relying on complex sets of rules and procedures that are difficult to remember. When it comes to the willingness component, the culture must promote resilience, and both managers and executives must give the impression that resilience is supported. This impression must be genuine; otherwise, employees will see right through it when their efforts do not work. Finally, HROs should develop the systems and processes that will support continuing learning as well as the expectations for it. This learning must be routine. Highly reliable teams do not wait for an incident to happen but rather use every opportunity to learn new information, even if they are not directly involved. Had this tenacity to learn been present in Three Mile Nuclear Plant's teams, they would have known about the problems with the valves. Efforts should be made towards creating new information, protecting organizational memory, and making sure that difficult lessons are never lost.

Only when a team has developed the features of high-reliability teams can individuals understand the individual pillars of HROs. The attributes of high-reliability teams presented in this chapter contain the essentials of each HRO principle. Understanding each principle is the next step, and the next chapter focuses on preoccupation with failure as the first principle of HROs.

Chapter 5

Preoccupation With Failure

Those that fail to learn from history are doomed to repeat it. –Winston Churchill

Under the first principle, there are three competencies that teams need to foster. Preoccupation with failure requires situational awareness so that small anomalies can be detected. Imagine that you are driving a car and hear an abnormal sound or feel minor vibrations when the brakes are applied. Chances are you will question if there is a problem and do further probing to find out what is going on. Problems always leave clues about the real problem. The clues are not always obvious, such as a vibration felt when the brakes are applied, and to be fully competent in this requires active monitoring. "The mindset that is preoccupied with failure looks for errors rather than assuming what is in front of them is correct" (Iorio, 2021). When teams are on the lookout for what is out of the ordinary, this hyper-vigilance leads to the early detection of small problems before they become too complicated to solve.

After the clues have been identified, teams need to anticipate what could potentially happen if the errors are ignored. This is where accountability plays a role, and employees with an HRO mindset know the consequences of ignoring clues to problems and speak out clearly without fear of reprisal. Characters such as Ed Pierson voiced their concerns about the 737 Max and even advocated for the factory to be closed even though the information available was incomplete, just like how the engineers of the Challenger implored NASA to delay the launch. It was this preoccupation with failure that led to these individuals recognizing that something was off and becoming relentless in finding a solution. This brings us to the third competency under this principle. When confronted with a problem, HROs understand that the information available is incomplete and seek to find out what it is that is unknown. This competence is the backbone of preoccupation with failure because it is persistent when it comes to finding out the causes of failure.

Benefits of Preoccupation With Failure

Improved Risk Management and Vigilance

This principle is the foundation of HRO behavior for good reasons. When teams are preoccupied with failure, the organization benefits from improved risk management, individuals are more attentive to small details, and there is enhanced learning, which leads to improved resilience. Risk management is improved because collectively, the organization becomes more vigilant and proactive when it comes to determining where the exposure is, and this leads to deliberate actions to find out things that are out of the ordinary. It is essential to keep the possible outcomes in mind so that attention is not wasted on things that are of no consequence. Over time, the teams will be able to determine what is critical and what is not by evaluating the possible outcomes of minor errors. Organizations become better at prioritizing what to focus on. A direct outcome of this vigilance is attention to detail, ultimately fostering careful planning as well as improved execution.

Increased Innovation

Since preoccupation with failure demands continuous probing, when small errors are noticed, organizations are guaranteed continuous learning and innovation. It is important to note that consistent innovation is only possible if there are adequate record-keeping and feedback mechanisms; otherwise, the lessons learned could be lost over time. As a manager, you will need to encourage reflection, and this could be done during meetings so that the lessons are learned collectively instead of being limited to a specific group of people investigating a problem. When lessons are learned, the organization becomes resilient as well. There is a phrase "once bitten, twice shy," and essentially, this means that when mistakes are made, important lessons are learned and usually avoided. The experiences, along with critical thinking and problem-solving acquired along the way, result in better anticipations and preparations against potential failures. This results in an organization that is better equipped to deal with unfamiliar situations and recover from these.

Counters Normalcy Bias

One more example of operations that observe preoccupation with failure is how the Navy does business. Navy personnel conduct what is called a "Foreign Object Debris" walk when an object goes missing on the deck. Something as simple as a tool used around the flight deck can bring everything to a halt until it is found. This activity is intended to sift through the vessel, particularly to scan and retrieve foreign objects and debris that could cause serious accidents. Regular scans also check for things that do not belong. Anything foreign is removed regardless of how small the piece is. If this is not done, what is out of place becomes a normal thing over time, increasing the risk of unsafe outcomes during normal operations. Normalcy bias is a cognitive bias that leads people to downplay threat warnings and can become a collective culture. Organizations in the process of adopting HRO principles should develop standard operating procedures that encourage employees to routinely be on the lookout for things that are not in place and threaten reliability.

Implementation Challenges

- **Can introduce other forms of bias:** If teams are not careful, preoccupation with failure can lead to confirmation bias based on what teams believe to be true. In certain circumstances, this can lead to an overestimation of favorable outcomes, while unfavorable outcomes are avoided. This confirmation bias can be a result of selective attention, memory bias, and interpretive bias. It often happens that when a team is focused on solving a problem, they are likely to selectively attend to information that confirms the worst-case scenario because the fear of failure is usually great, especially when the stakes are high. When there is a problem, and there is fear of failure, teams can overlook positive signs and focus on the negatives. In the case of interpretive bias, information that is ambiguous or has dual meanings can lead teams down the wrong path. Memory can also lead to bias in that information that supports what is already known can be looked at with prejudice. The danger here is that failure-related anxiety can lead to remembering previous failures more vividly than past achievements, which can defeat the purpose of preoccupation with failure. Interpretation bias results when ambiguous information is presented in a manner that confirms preoccupation with failure.

- **Fixation:** Another problem with a preoccupation with failure is fixation. One example to consider is the crash of Eastern Airlines Lockheed L1011, where the captain was concerned that the nose landing gear was not down and locked in place because the indicator light was not showing this. In the end, the aircraft ran out of altitude while the plane was in a holding pattern as the crew was trying to verify whether the gear was down or not. The crew did perform the test to confirm that the gear was down, but they simply did not accept that this was just the light that was faulty. This fixation led to the crew forgetting to monitor their altitude because they were all focused on solving the problem. Following the crash, the investigations determined that the gear was indeed down, but the light bulb was blown. Similarly, when teams are preoccupied with failure, it is possible that too much focus can be placed on solving trivial problems, leaving the bigger picture unattended. The crash of Eastern Airlines Lockheed L1011 was one of the main accidents that led to the industry-wide adoption of Crew Resource Management. From this, we can learn how organizations should successfully implement preoccupation with failure. Fixation is more likely to occur when there have been similar failures in the past. When there is a problem that needs to be solved with consistent probing, there must be a monitoring team that is focused on the bigger picture to ensure that both attention and resources are still allocated to what is needed to keep operations running.

Successfully Developing Preoccupation With Failure Mindset

Organizations that have a large organogram have two or three people with clearly defined authority under a section manager. Senior managers should encourage floor-level managers to be open with teams to get constructive feedback. A team member must be able to tell those in a more senior position that their approach is risking the operation. The reason is that even if the official policy allows people to speak up, it can be difficult to do so in real time. Operations sensitive to time, such as a flight, are an example of this, and a captain who approached the flight deck with an attitude that tells the junior officers to speak up if they notice out-of-the-ordinary behavior from them provides an environment fertile for people to actually speak up. It usually takes a great deal of courage for a junior employee to tell a senior or more experienced employee that what they are doing is wrong or dangerous. Making this clear at the beginning of an operation will make teamwork more effective when one person outranks the other. One more example is the crash of *Hapag-Lloyd Flight 3378*. In this incident, the crew took off with an extended landing gear, leading to a higher-than-normal fuel burn because of increased drag. In this case, the first officer was aware that the plane would run out of fuel and would not reach the destination based on the performance charts.

Individuals can become more preoccupied with failure by developing situational awareness. The key action is to understand what the data is communicating. This should be followed by an inquiry into which data is lacking and how it can be found. Despite the first officer's insight, there was no strong or forceful emphasis to alert the captain that things would go out of hand. Further suggestions to land at an alternative airport were fruitless, and the crew proceeded with the initial plan. Perhaps the outcome would have been different had the first officer made it clear to the captain that the fuel would not be enough and explained the reasoning behind his distrust of the flight management system instead of passively accepting the captain's decisions. For the junior employee, when hints that something is not right do not work, it is better to say what needs to be said directly and clearly for operations to become reliable and safe.

Preoccupation With Failure vs. Risk

Despite the two concepts being closely related, the focus, actions involved, and impression of control of preoccupation with risk and preoccupation with failure are different. Overall, preoccupation with risk gives teams a sense of control over the outcome, while preoccupation with failure can have the opposite effect. Let's consider the case of the Bhopal Chemical disaster: The operators and managers should have been concerned about the potential of a gas leak since preoccupation with failure focuses on the likely negative outcomes given a specific situation. On the contrary, preoccupation with risk focuses more on the potential outcomes in general, taking the anomalies into consideration. For the Challenger disaster, there was no certainty of what exactly would go wrong and when. The engineers were simply concerned about the possible outcomes should the O-rings fail in cold weather. Of course, the engineers had an idea that a failure would be catastrophic given the test data and the nature of the operation, but an accident like this had not happened before, and the concerns were only based on a thorough understanding of the materials involved.

The two concepts also differ when it comes to the emotional responses they come with. Often, when people are preoccupied with failure, there is more anxiety, fear of the unknown, and, at times, doubt when the information available is not complete. On the other hand, when risk is a concern, tasks are approached with caution, and the emotions associated include being guarded and on high alert. Put yourself in the shoes of the engineers and scientists working on the Challenger; the circumstances they were faced with when identifying and managing would lead to the actions taken. It is likely that they were preoccupied with the possibilities of what could happen should the seals fail. This leads to a difference in the actions taken between teams that are preoccupied with risk and failure. If not carefully managed, preoccupation with failure can lead to avoidance behavior, as individuals may be hesitant to take risks or try new things out of fear of failure. In the case of the Bhopal disaster, preoccupation with failure likely led to avoidance behavior among plant workers and managers, and in the end, no action was taken. Individuals who are preoccupied with risk-taking are proactive in reducing risk and conducting tests, simulations, and other risk assessment and management exercises with the goal of coming up with workarounds. For the Challenger disaster, the engineers took proactive action, which included developing a backup plan for the shuttle's safe return should something fail.

In short, preoccupation with failure warrants continuous attention to abnormalities that may be signs of more serious issues within the system. As a result, teams must put in a lot of effort to find any small and new failures since they might be a sign of bigger ones elsewhere in the system. HROs put a lot of effort into planning ahead and identifying critical errors that they don't want to make. Finally, HROs are aware that people's understanding of the circumstances, the surrounding area, and their own group is limited. When people search for failures, they admit that their knowledge isn't complete and work from this assumption to understand the issue more. This is critical because doubt can be useful to uncover more information that is not immediately apparent.

Chapter 6

Reluctance to Simplify Interpretations

E *nergy and persistence conquer all things.*
   –Benjamin Franklin

The persistence that comes from being preoccupied with failure builds on to the second principle that is characteristic of all HROs. There are no simple explanations for a problem when it comes to HROs. Incidents and anomalies are viewed in the context of the complexity of the operations, and both managers and teams refuse to excuse failures without thorough investigation. We see this in the airline industry whenever an aircraft goes down, and whenever there is a probable cause, it is looked at thoroughly, and the pieces are put together until the evidence is conclusive. At times, the evidence can be overwhelming but misleading, and organizations that do not want to get hit again must check if the cause of the problem is the correct diagnosis.

Exceptional reliability is achieved when hidden factors that might increase the likelihood of unreliable performance are brought to the surface. This is because categorizing a problem or applying a blanket reason to an outcome might conceal contradicting information. While categories are layers that help us understand, they can also mask small details that might signal unforeseen issues. This means that when a problem happens, the full sequence of events leading to an undesirable outcome might be ignored, and only the seemingly obvious contributors are addressed. Organizing a team or operation with the reluctance to simplify in mind requires encouraging process diversity, argumentation openness, and the ability and willingness to take action in order to understand.

Assessing the Organization's Practices

Individuals responsible for creating an environment that is "reluctant to simplify" need to make an assessment of how teams approach problem-solving. This can be done by taking note of the extent to which teams take things for granted and looking at whether asking questions is encouraged at every level in the organization. You can make it into a checklist, and possible questions for this are:

- Do people pay close attention to one another? Is it common for people to have their opinions rejected?

- Do we help everyone, no matter their position or status, improve their interpersonal skills?

- Do people here respect skeptics? Do we try to change the way things are now?

- Do people spend more time analyzing a situation rather than simply arguing for their preconceived notions when something unexpected occurs?

- Do individuals treat one another with a lot of respect, regardless of their position or power within the organization?

Reluctance to Simplify Best Practices

For HROs to be true to the definition, they also need to survive the modern business environment. When evidence points to a different problem or something that is unsolvable, it is essential that teams recognize this and be taught to adapt and change course because it is futile to try and beat a dead horse. When confronted with a particular problem, daily briefings are necessary to share important information on the situation for collective decision-making. If team building and training exercises are implemented, managers need to:

- **Emphasize multidisciplinary teams:** The benefit here is that organizations can get diverse views on problems or risks to reliability. This makes the organization better at understanding how to approach the problem and reduces the likelihood of getting too lost in avoiding the simplification of a problem. When diverse experience and skills are combined, more ideas are available to determine what the cause of a problem is, similar to how the NTSB investigates accidents that are complex, and at times, they do this by involving teams from other organizations. If you recall the example regarding the experience where further probing revealed that the pressure vessel needed fixing, getting to the right solution was a result of coordination between multidisciplinary teams with engineers external to the organization included. A more thorough understanding of the problems at hand is made possible by the distinct knowledge and abilities that each team member brings to the table.

One more important factor is to make sure that the ground is even. Getting people with diverse experiences and expertise to agree is quite difficult, and this plays into the hands of reluctance to simplify. Since HROs work in constantly changing circumstances, multidisciplinary teams resist the urge to simplify, and when the optimum solution is found, the reaction times to unique problems are exceptional. It is critical that the team members are treated equally to encourage the expression of different viewpoints. If everyone is on the same page, multidisciplinary teams make communication easier by giving people from various fields a place to work together, discuss ideas, and gain new perspectives. This cross-disciplinary cooperation increases the quality and clarity of communication while lowering conflicts and boosting coordination.

The last benefit is the elimination of blind spots. This is possible because multidisciplinary teams contribute to reducing blind spots by encouraging a thorough examination of complex systems, identifying interdependencies, and uncovering potential vulnerabilities. Ultimately, there is robust problem-solving because different knowledge from several disciplines is brought together in real time to develop creative and efficient solutions to issues. This strategy improves the organization's capacity for general problem-solving.

- **Generate hypotheses about what is going on:** For multidisciplinary teams to work, there must be a foundation from which to start problem-solving. Specialized teams within the area of focus need to have a set of hypotheses or theories for problem-solving. Frontline managers and supervisors must know how to create the bigger picture and make deliberate steps to create complete pictures to "see more." Doing this will help teams understand the long-term and system-wide consequences of proposed actions. If there is a hypothesis to work from, it becomes easier to streamline the problems to their roots and develop the action plan for each identified issue or probable cause.

- **Take advantage of scientific tools:** *Failure Mode and Effects Analysis* (FMEA), as well as *Root Cause Analysis* (RCA), are examples of proven tools that teams can use to be certain that the cause of the problem is correctly identified. For specific and unique problems, multidisciplinary teams can face barriers when certain team members have more expertise and experience than the rest of the team. Problem-finding tools ensure a more accurate understanding of the issue and that the possible outcomes are identified within a short time frame while eliminating quick generalizations. In addition to this, the tools assist companies in taking into account the problems that exist inside the system and promote looking at the larger context, organizational factors, and underlying processes that may affect the development or persistence of problems. Core causes are addressed as opposed to just the symptoms and detecting systemic flaws or associated issues. This makes the quality of the data used in problem-solving important, and teams must be committed to collecting as much relevant data as possible; otherwise, it may take longer to reach a solution. If the data is incorrect, the risk is that the wrong solution might be proposed, and this is an important link between preoccupation with failure and the reluctance to simplify. RCA and FMEA work better to uncover the root causes of issues when they are presented with accurate data. The tools themselves encourage the use of reliable data to produce evidence-based assessments. In order to refine the understanding of complicated situations or incorporate new information, RCA, in particular, emphasizes the significance of reviewing and reevaluating earlier assessments. These iterative methods lead to further refinement in finding the best solution to achieving reliability.

Dangers of Reluctance to Simplify

- **Overcomplication, leading to poor resource allocation and coordination:** Sometimes, reluctance to simplify is not a good idea because there is a risk of keeping an organization stuck in an endless loop of problem-solving. A good example to illustrate this is Nokia, which, up until the middle of the 2000s, had the biggest market share of the mobile phone market. New competition with simpler business models, such as Apple, left Nokia behind because, in essence, they were stuck in the old way of doing things. The writing was on the wall that touchscreen smartphones were the future, and Nokia, like Blackberry, initially resisted embracing the simplicity and user-friendly design that these devices offered. The business stuck with its conventional operating system and design concepts, which were outmoded in the quickly developing mobile market. This strategy produced a complicated and fragmented product range, leading to higher production costs along with a complex supply chain, making it challenging to adapt to shifting consumer expectations. In addition, Nokia's organizational structure featured a number of regional divisions and business units, each of which had its own decision-making procedures and strategies. In the end, it became difficult to coordinate efforts and react to market changes because of this decentralized structure. Nokia finally grasped the necessity for change, although it took some time. The same can be said for any organization, regardless of the business operation or area of activity. Managers need to be aware that sometimes simplicity can be a good thing and need to understand the limits of reluctance to simplify.

The last example shows that organizations need to set limits when it comes to this principle. Achieving order and clarity and creating routines inside an organization both require simplification, which is crucial. However, it's important to be careful when simplifying things too much or quickly because doing so might lead to significant information being missed, which could be crucial information needed for problem-solving. Complex operations need to find balance when it comes to this principle. Consider the Columbia Space Shuttle disaster as well. The accident happened because a piece of foam breached the wing of the spacecraft after falling off from the spacecraft's external tank, specifically the bipod ramp. This had been a known problem for several years, and NASA had already labeled this issue as an "in-family" problem to indicate that this issue was known. The significance of the problem was reduced because the resulting damage was classified as a minor "tile problem" at the maintenance level when the impact was actually quite severe.

Additionally, the "cultural traits and organizational practices detrimental to safety were allowed to develop" with "reliance on past success as a substitute for sound engineering practices" (Dobrijevic & Howell, 2023). Organizations that are reluctant to simplify, however, can increase their chances of solving a problem once and for all without wasting resources or compromising reliability. When there is a problem, the goal is to provide the right solution the first time because there is a risk of applying the wrong fix, which can drain significant resources while leaving the organization with the same exposure before the fix. You could imagine the outcome had the Three Mile

Nuclear incident been incorrectly diagnosed. This would be another disaster waiting to happen with possibly more serious consequences than the first.

Chapter 7

Sensitivity to Operations

C omplex operations have a lot of moving parts, and this makes coordination important. The third principle building on the previous two is sensitivity to operations. Sensitivity to operations is about what is happening right now, regardless of the protocols. One key component needed for effective coordination is information, which must be provided to the teams when needed in a concise manner. Overloading teams with too much information can lead to weak signals pointing to a problem being missed, making preoccupation with failure useless. Organizations that are sensitive to operations give employees the right information when it is needed so that they can focus on the practical and operational aspects. Time is of the essence, and when there is an update to operations, it is critical that this information is communicated as quickly as possible. Standard

operating procedures (SOPs) need to be updated
as well, and there must be a verification that all
employees are aware of the changes, no matter
how small. Again, we will consider an example in
the aviation industry to illustrate the significance
of this. *Varig Flight 254* crashed in September
1989 because it headed in the wrong direction and
eventually ran out of fuel. The company changed
how the headings are represented from three digits
to four digits while the captain was on vacation, and
this led to an incorrect interpretation of the flight
plan. It took a combination of a seemingly minor
update and an unaware captain for the accident to
occur. This can happen in any complex operation,
and when you think about the operations in your
organization, you can easily notice how one missed
minor update can lead to catastrophe.

For organizations to demonstrate operational
sensitivity, attention must be paid to the reality
that exists inside their operations. Employees could
unknowingly believe that their actions correspond
to the expectations and good practice as a result
of typical procedures. These assumptions usually
lead to a misconception of security or reliability
that hides failure from being recognized. In the
case of Varig Flight 254, the captain only noticed
that the aircraft was in the wrong place when
the airport could not be located when descending
for the landing approach. You will need to drive

your organization towards stressing the actual work rather than intentions and characterize this work by looking at the relationships and interdependencies of different operations rather than its pieces. Routine work must be looked at carefully, simplified, and made clear. Regardless of how small a change to routine work appears, it must be communicated. Refrain from making complex changes but rather make incremental changes to SOPs unless something is critical to the reliability of operations. Radical and complex changes decrease understanding and coordination and lead to teams that are disconnected from the organization's goals of making the change in the first place. Continuous operations that involve a big group of personnel can survive a large number of minor changes in how things are done because the checks and balances in place make it less likely that one failure can lead to unforeseen interactions with other changes and complete failure. The overarching competence for sensitivity to operations is accountability from both a human and system perspective.

Sensitivity to Operations vs. Planning

Organizations that are not HRO-oriented make the mistake of being sensitive to planning. In the majority of cases, planning focuses on intentions rather than how the actual work will be done to achieve the intended reliability. Of course, no organization can exist without planning; otherwise, operations will not move at all. When the planning is being done, it must be looked at holistically, with the operator on the floor in mind. A hospital, for example, might need to make sure that the approach to work puts more emphasis on checking if the equipment is ready before a surgical procedure rather than planning or discussing how procedures are carried out. Achieving the right balance takes time and coordinated efforts, but the key is to understand the connections within the system regardless of the industry.

The ability to predict the possibilities becomes important for an organization to be sensitive to operations. Complex operations that are dynamic need people who are able to use predictive approaches in real time. One action can seem to be the right intervention when things are going wrong, but at times, the correct action can have undesired consequences, and this requires people who are able to analyze events in real time and look at the possibilities. Rarely do dynamic situations allow for planning because remedial action is often required immediately. This is the reason transparency and clear communication are critical, and all barriers to information flow must be eliminated. If possible, develop systems that allow real time feedback, especially when things are not working. Organizations that have several divisions need these divisions to have autonomy for the organization to be sensitive to operations. Centralized decision-making can lead to missed opportunities for correcting things before they get out of hand.

People are responsible for decision-making instead of organizations, as commonly thought. Decentralized decision-making for real time problems in the field can help an organization maximize its reliability, especially when the main decision-makers in the organization are not easy to access or have other pressing issues to focus on. Organizations can be bombarded with one problem after another, and this is where high-reliability teams shine. While centralized decision-making can facilitate standardized approaches to operations and make it easy to allocate resources, time-sensitive operations benefit more when decisions are left to the individual divisions. As long as no rules are broken, making a decision, no matter how imperfect, is better than no decision at all. Over time, teams will learn how to make decisions that best address a specific situation, which can be further refined by decision-making models.

Decision Making and HROs

The "Observe, Orient, Decide, and Act" model, otherwise known as the OODA loop, is a useful decision-making tool that HROs rely on when confronted with unfamiliar and dynamic problems in real time. Although the general approach is to start by observing what is going on, it doesn't really matter where one actually starts on the decision loop because a problem may present itself differently. Looking at the model from the generic approach, the "observe" step involves looking at the situation and gathering information about what is going on. The data must be accurately collected to understand the problem properly. This data is analyzed so that there is orientation, leading to a mental picture that makes sense of the observed information. At this stage, the possible outcomes and risks will already be apparent, at least partially. Based on the picture that is available, a decision can be made. This decision can be preliminary, especially when there is continuous evaluation of the situation. Sometimes, it is not possible to keep evaluating the situation, so the decision maker needs to make every effort to ensure that the decision is sound because it is not always possible to walk back on the initial decision.

The decision-making should be quick, considering the time sensitivity often associated with OODA, but also well-informed based on the observations and orientation stages. Once the decision has been made, it is time for action, which simply involves implementing what has been decided. The cycle begins again until there is satisfaction that the issue has been resolved and nothing has been missed. OODA can be implemented at the individual level, but it is more effective when teams do it. Organizations that allow decentralized decision-making benefit from increased utilization of local knowledge because high-reliability teams have the knowledge and expertise since they are the closest to the operations.

Developing a Sensitive Culture

Mindfulness is the secret to developing a culture that is sensitive to operations. Frontline employees, in particular, need to keep their eye on the ball throughout because this is where things usually go wrong first. When there is a high level of presence of mind during an ongoing operation, responses to anomalies happen quickly, and split-second decisions can make a difference. Look at a surgical procedure, for instance. When there is excessive bleeding, the first instinct of a mindful surgeon is to block the leak, which can even include using the fingers while calling out for an instrument intended for this purpose. When teams are mindful, there is a sixth sense that kicks in to adapt to what is going on in the moment.

Naturally, collective mindfulness becomes the pillar of organizational sensitivity to operations. For the manager, it is important to know who is doing what and where more than what is actually going on. Consider a scenario where an organization is dealing with a sensitive process that must be sterile and needs only authorized personnel to be present in the facility. In the Navy, different colored shirts are used to distinguish personnel by role. You can easily transfer this to your own organization with identifiers such as restricted access badges and real time monitoring of access. This eliminates the possibility of unauthorized people being where they should not be, even if they are part of the organization. Sometimes, it is not about the sensitive nature of the process, but access to sensitive data should also be taken seriously by an organization that seeks to develop exceptional sensitivity to operations. Operators and frontline employees should place more emphasis on what is actually happening with the process and data. The research conducted by Roth and Mullen is an important study explaining the importance of situational awareness at every level of operations and how communications or relationships impact situational awareness.

The research looked at decision-making at the operator's level during a simulated nuclear power plant emergency similar to the Three Mile Nuclear incident discussed earlier. When operators used shared mental models and group story-building to construct several levels of situational awareness during the simulated emergencies, they were able to maintain dependability in ever-changing circumstances. The more they shared and validated, the more situational awareness they developed. The operators did more than merely be aware of the circumstance. To determine whether the instructions in the processes made sense in the particular circumstances of the occurrence, they created narratives. They used their knowledge of the presumptions and logic underpinning the processes to deal with situations that such procedures did not completely cover. They continuously evaluated whether observed plant activity was consistent with known factors or if it pointed to an unforeseen failure. In the end, operators who were fully aware of what was going on were able to restore plant function to safe levels in less time than operators who did not have a higher degree of situational awareness.

Barriers to Sensitivity

When a team or operation involves experienced individuals, especially those who have been with the organization for a good number of years, it is easy for ignorance to seep into the operations.

There is always more to learn, and even the most experienced can encounter trouble if they are unaware of the danger. Another barrier is a casual approach to sensitive operations. Again, the risk of this is also higher in seasoned employees because the job is taken as a routine operation, which can lead to corners being cut. Situational awareness is thrown out of the window, and when something goes wrong, the important clues would have been missed in the beginning.

Managers should be alarmed when teams and individuals make comments such as "It didn't look this serious" because they show a lack of understanding of the underlying causes of poor reliability. Comments like these also signal that clues are not being taken seriously. Potentially, this could be a result of team members becoming too confident in the processes, leading to complacency and shortcuts. Compare this behavior with how new and relatively junior employees are often quick to react when something is out of the ordinary and do better at reporting abnormalities because they are unsure of what the indications mean.

Leadership Responsibilities

Managers need to train teams to think on their feet and be able to correct errors in real time and reinforce this at every level in the organization to remove barriers that can make an organization insensitive to operations. Doing this will go a long way to ensure that situational awareness is integrated into how the organization does things. Audits can be useful to identify areas of improvement, and this can require asking questions such as:

- Do employees in our organization interact with one another frequently enough to have a clear understanding of the challenges they encounter on a daily basis?

- Is someone with the power to act accessible to those on the front lines at times of high activity or when issues arise?

- Do our organization's leaders closely monitor daily activities?

- Are people familiar with activities outside of their field of expertise?

- Do people proactively seek input on situations that aren't working out?

- Do people have access to resources in case unforeseen circumstances arise?

The questions provide an opportunity to correct approaches to work that can result in the floor manager or the operator being unaware of what is going on around them. Once there is a complete understanding of how people approach operations, it is critical to have someone with decision-making authority right on the ground where the action is in case a split-second decision is needed. Regular staff huddles are also important to keep everyone in the loop of what is going on, even if there hasn't been a major event or update. Although sensitivity to operations focuses on real time situational awareness and decision-making, adaptation must also be done within the framework of the SOPs because these are usually proven procedures that result in standardized work to mitigate errors, reduce undesired variability, and identify opportunities for improvement. Going back to the example of Varig Flight 254, the accident could have been easily avoided if the first officer had informed the captain that he had made a mistake according to the new procedures because the first officer was present when the changes were made. It is critical to encourage:

- Reporting deviations from expected performance.

- Early identification of problems so actions can be taken before the problems become substantial. Another contributing factor to the crash of *Varig 254* is that the deviation from the plan was identified late into the flight. There were a number of clues, such as the position of the sun in the sky during take-off, which the captain should have identified since he was familiar with the route.

- Ongoing concern with the unexpected.

- Organizational activities that build trust. This is key because refusing to speak up out of fear of punishment creates a system that knows less than necessary to remain effective.

- All members of the organization have a big picture of the current operations.

Operationalizing Sensitivity

Your teams need to be able to distinguish between operations that are normal and the ones that are "high-tempo" to develop adaptive risk perception. High-tempo operations are dynamic and often have a lot of moving parts, increasing the chances of something going wrong. However, it will take a combination of many small errors for something to go catastrophically wrong. Let's use our usual example of a flight to illustrate how dynamic one operation can be. When an emergency happens, cases that have all the markers of an HRO involve more than the flight crew. The cabin crew plays an equally pivotal role in ensuring that everything goes smoothly. The tempo in the flight deck and cabin differ, as well as the complexity of the tasks throughout the flight between the two groups in the same operation. Your organization must be able to look at the operations from the same lens and tailor-make reliability and safety expectations for each unit. Provide clear signals of the operating modes. There must be clear signs that indicate which mode is operational, and additionally, the organization needs to conduct regular refresher training on what to do in each operating mode.

Chapter 8

Consequences of Human Error

*L*ife doesn't get easier or more forgiving, we get
stronger and more resilient. –Steve Maraboli

Another feature that sets HROs apart is the
consequences of human error, upon which
organizational resilience is built. High-reliability
cultures enable organizations to quickly contain
faults and continue operating in the face of
setbacks. In order to respond effectively when
system failures do occur, leaders and staff need to
be taught to make quick situational assessments
and know that failure to do so can have
repercussions. This does not mean that people
are punished for mistakes, although appropriate
disciplinary measures still need to be applied
to discourage negligence. On the contrary, the
individual or team that makes a mistake must
be accountable for it and given the opportunity
to fix it. People who learn from their mistakes

are better positioned to fix the error because painful lessons offer fertile ground for learning what works and what does not. Distinctions need to be made between process failure and human failure. When people make mistakes, they must be held accountable for their actions while taking note of system flaws and separating these flaws from human action. All events threatening an organization's reliability or safety begin with an initiating event, which is a result of either equipment failure or human error. This could be influenced by external events as well, and if the initiating event is not interrupted, then the outcome is likely hazardous to the operations or products. It is possible for the same initiating event to occur repeatedly without incident, thus termed "initiating event frequency," which is the reason behind the importance of reluctance to simplify and preoccupation with failure. Most initiating events are known or can be predicted, but preoccupation with failure is useful to catch potential initiating events before an incident occurs.

Individual and Team Resilience

Team resilience is built when the relationship between the organization and employees is mutual and fair. A commitment to resilience involves constructing systems reliably while considering human factors. They make it hard to do the wrong thing and easy to do the right. A culture of tolerance is the core pillar of commitment to resilience, and according to Ferrazzi, Race, and Vincent (2021), four essentials are needed to build a tolerant culture for an organization that seeks to commit to resilience. The pillars are candor, resourcefulness, empathy, and humility.

Creating Organizational Tolerance

Big organizations can afford tolerance towards trivial deviations at the individual level because the system must be immune to a single point of failure. From this perspective, organizations must use trivial errors as coaching opportunities, and this is where empathy comes in. When people genuinely care about each other in the work environment, the outcome is co-elevation, which seeks to bring out the best in each individual with collective excellence in mind. The team is more important compared to individual success and progress. For this to work, the team must be open to each other and speak truthfully about any operational challenges at the individual level. For critical operations that are restricted to a small team, it is necessary for people who are not sure what they are doing to speak out and seek assistance or relinquish their responsibilities until there is confidence that the right thing is being done. This also requires humility for everyone involved, and a senior employee should be able to approach a junior employee for guidance on things that they may not know. Technological advancements are one area where an expert can be lacking compared to a recent graduate. Even if the underlying process remains the same, improvements in instrumentation, process control, and automation can bring challenges even to the most senior members of a team. Overall, resilience is built when teams approach their limitations with resourcefulness, considering each member as a possible source of operational stability.

Simplifying Processes

The more complex something is, the less likely it is to be successful. When processes are simplified, they become easy to follow because of enhanced clarity and agility. Simple processes are also easier to teach, making training and continual development programs cost-effective and easier to implement, reducing cognitive load. It is likely that when a process requires too much focus or is difficult to do, employees may deviate from following instructions, which presents opportunities for mistakes. If there are fewer things to remember and the things that need remembering are simpler, people are less prone to make mistakes, leading to a better commitment to resilience. Employees are better able to comprehend their tasks and react to unforeseen occurrences as a result of the decreased errors and misunderstandings. If you are familiar with the *Hudson Miracle* story, you can easily relate to the importance of keeping things simple to deal with complicated problems. In an interview after the first-ever successful water landing of an airline in history, the pilot recalled the events, highlighting that he simply adapted what he knew to solve an unfamiliar problem (Goswami, 2019). By making it possible to respond quickly to changing conditions, you empower teams to recover effectively from setbacks because of increased flexibility. One direct outcome of simple processes is a common understanding of operations and adherence to established standards, leading to better standardization. This makes it easier to implement SOPs that are relevant to the organization and team. Process simplification also gives organizations room to make improvements and get rid of things that do not work, boosting resilience all around. Employees can concentrate on important activities and make quicker, more accurate decisions when the complexity is lower.

Reducing Autonomy

Autonomy results in decision-making that relies on personal preference or individualized beliefs, leading to variations in outcomes. Reliability that is resilient requires organizations to set the expectation that operations need to follow using evidence-based best practices unless there are conditions that prevent standardized practices from being observed. You will notice that whenever a big job needs to be done, teams that rely on debriefs, checklists, and clear communication seem to have no complications on the job. No one really decides what they want to do without checking with the team if the intended action deviates from the standardized procedures. Reducing autonomy within teams in the context of an HRO can help build resilience by promoting adherence to best practices, leading to coordinated situational awareness that enables teams to effectively respond to unexpected events and maintain a high level of safety. By reducing autonomy and emphasizing best practices and communication, HROs can enhance their teams' ability to respond effectively and maintain resilience in complex and high-risk environments.

Highlight Deviations From Practice

Sometimes, employees may use rationale to depart from established procedures for good reason. Organizations should foster conditions where workers can use their knowledge wisely and deviate from procedures when necessary, but they should also diligently record those deviations for later study. Once the new information has been reviewed, it may be possible to change the methodology or educate teams to increase reliability. A case in point is the "Miracle on the Hudson" flight, where the crew went against the procedure of trying to head to the nearest airport, opting to land on the river instead. This deviation from the conventional practice of finding an available runway was prompted by their assessment of the situation, including the loss of engine power and the limited time available for decision-making. While the initial official investigations suggested that the crew did not do the right thing, the evidence was overwhelming to support their decision. Choosing to deviate from standard procedures after evaluating the situation contributed to an outcome where all 155 passengers walked away.

The medical field also has unique examples of deviations from practice. A common activity before an operation is what is known as a "surgical time-out." Before the operation is carried out, the team takes a time-out to verify critical information such as blood type, confirm where the surgery will be conducted, along with potential patient-specific needs for the procedure. If an unanticipated problem or discrepancy is discovered during a time-out, the surgical team may deviate from the set procedure and take the necessary measures to resolve the issue. For instance, the team might change the original plan and make revisions to prevent utilizing an allergic medication if a patient's medical records reveal a previously undetected allergy to a drug that was intended for use. Even though time-outs are a part of the protocol, the surgical team's ability to deviate from the plan to deal with unforeseen problems is an excellent example of the value of adaptability and flexibility in high-reliability healthcare organizations. When carried out with consideration for the safety and well-being of the patient, these deviations help to increase the overall reliability and efficiency of the service.

Layer of Protection Analysis (LOPA)

Making the weakest link in the operations resilient also contributes to a resilient organization. For this to work, an evaluation needs to be made to determine the weakest link and how this weakness compromises the organization, especially when there are multiple layers of protection in place. The

Bhopal incident is a classic case of zero resilience because none of the protective measures were working on the day of the disaster. According to Sibilski (2020), the plant originally had six layers of protection which were:

- 1st layer: Process design and plant operation philosophy

- 2nd layer: Temperature control

- 3rd layer: Critical alarms and response

- 4th layer: Plant automation

- 5th layer: Relief system

- 6th layer: Flare

- 7th layer: Emergency response

Without going into the details of the sequence, everything but the 5th layer failed, leading to the gas release into the atmosphere. This case would have been avoided if the plant had a comprehensive layer of protection analysis or LOPA, which is "a method of analyzing the likelihood of a harmful outcome event based on an initiating event frequency and on the probability of failure of a series of independent layers of protection capable of preventing the harmful outcome" (Nolan, 2019). When conducting LOPA, the assessment needs to be measured against the company's risk tolerance criteria. Operations are not abandoned if they are above the organizational risk tolerance. Rather, an additional layer must be evaluated and added to the system so that the operations are resilient. Some activities might actually be impossible to abandon and compel an organization to find ways to mitigate risk. For example, in hospitals, doctors do not back out of surgeries when they have already been started. If things don't go to plan, surgeons counter unexpected situations by developing contingencies. LOPA assessments can be outsourced because they need to be done correctly, but in general, they involve establishing the risk tolerance criteria, identifying hazards, and setting boundaries, as well as identifying initiating events and the associated frequencies.

Scenario Planning

At the center of building a resilient team and system is scenario planning. The objective is to assess the severity of possible scenarios, assess the likelihood of something happening, and assess the risk itself. This scenario planning must be integrated across the entire organization, and coordinating this activity throughout the organization is the first step to deference to expertise, which will be discussed in the next chapter. Once the risks and possibilities have been identified and prioritized, operations need to be standardized through procedures that ensure people always carry out the same action in the same manner. Standardization makes it simpler to teach employees about the procedures and facilitates clear signals when processes fail. This can help the organization to develop and implement effective reforms.

Organizational Fluidity

Resilient systems require fluidity because it enables them to modify their structures in response to both internal and external pressures. To live and prosper, resilient systems take on a variety of structures and forms, and their enduring relationships can adapt to changes. In order to be resilient, an organization must be able to quickly change its organizational structures in the face of adversity rather than depending only on hierarchy and centralized autonomy. The Challenger accident serves as a prime example of the lack of fluidity, as the failure was caused by weak links, a lack of mutual trust, and a lack of collaborative problem-solving techniques. Successful HROs and resilient systems, on the other hand, display flexibility by routinely rebuilding themselves, updating their beliefs, and changing their expectations. They don't stick to outdated organizational practices and instead embrace change. Organizations can develop fluidity in several ways.

Grabowski and Roberts (2019) suggest developing solid social networks and ties with other groups, either by growing their network connections or forming coalitions, as one way to build organizational fluidity. Networking and collaboration offer organizations the opportunity to learn from each other as well as allow a group to scale or downsize operations with little compromise in response to outside factors or perceived dangers. The emphasis of HROs is on strong and equal relationships between members to encourage efficient information sharing and cooperative problem-solving, all of which reduce risks. By switching between centralized and decentralized structures depending on the circumstance, HROs demonstrate fluidity, enabling them to react swiftly to changing conditions.

Chapter 9

Recognizing the Value of Knowledge

When people talk, listen completely. —Ernest Hemingway

Arguably, the greatest benefit for an organization that has accountability that cascades down from the top to the bottom is ownership. HROs do not spend time playing politics about seniority when there is a problem to solve. Instead, they understand that employees with the most pertinent knowledge to fix a problem may not necessarily be the most senior team member or have the highest title in the room. Each member of the team is valued and is a potential problem solver. Deference to expertise is the capstone principle that HROs base their success on, and the driver of this is decision-making from the top. The principle encourages employees and safety teams to listen and respond to situations regardless of rank, position, or title. This is exactly what happened in the example of the experience discussed in the first chapter. Of course, a lot of options had already been explored to fix the facility after the new equipment was installed, but the mere fact that the management was open to allowing an engineer out of college who was new at the company to propose a solution to a multi-million dollar problem is evidence of deference to expertise. The answer could have been simply no, but because of the organization's deference to expertise, everyone was open to proposing solutions to problems if the approach could be justified. In the end, a solution was found, and the facility began to operate within the design parameters.

A direct opposite of this outcome is the Challenger Disaster. One of the engineers on the program, Roger Boisjoly, warned about the potential dangers associated with the O-rings but was ignored. The engineer, along with a small group of other experts, repeatedly raised concerns about the seals' inability to withstand cold temperatures and the chances that they would fail. However, because there were other senior members on the side of NASA and Morton Thiokol, the warnings were downplayed. According to the evidence after the crash of the shuttle, Roger Boisjoly and the other engineers were excluded from a meeting that gave the green light to the launch (Ware, 2016). Earlier on, the importance of decision-making on the floor to react to dynamic errors was discussed. When it comes to deference to expertise, decision-making is equally important, and there must be consensus on the right decision. Even if one person in the room does not agree, their reasoning for the objections must be thoroughly looked at because consensus looks at what the majority wants, even if there is poor evaluation of the issues. For deference to expertise to work, there needs to be someone who is ready to offer a solution. This is why there must be a cultural shift on the floor. Regular employees with no decision-making authority or rank should make themselves heard, no matter the cost when it comes to issues concerning public safety and reliability.

Operationalizing Deference to Expertise

Transparency

Establish patterns of decision-making that filter people with the right knowledge by increasing employee engagement and overcoming consensus. By making the decision-making process visible, employees will soon know that anyone is allowed to present their ideas. In order to be transparent with decisions, your decision-making on important issues in the organization and things that relate to reliability should be explained, with the rationale behind given. The decision itself might not be popular, but if people understand why things need to be done a certain way, confidence grows for employees who also use rationale when trying to solve problems. The decisions themselves need to involve several experts who, in turn, are also transparent with their juniors. Not everyone needs to be in the meeting room, but if the leadership has a culture of transparency, this encourages the whole organization to be more forthcoming.

Since communication is a two-way street, when managers communicate decisions that have been made, they should ask those under them to share their thoughts. For valid concerns, there should be evidence that these have been factored into the decision. Failure to do this can send a message that dissent is not welcome and feedback is not valued. Collaboration on problem-solving becomes easier with transparency. Organizations can access the collective intelligence of their workforce by sharing information and enlisting pertinent expertise. This cooperative strategy encourages people to respect others' knowledge, appreciate the value of many viewpoints, and cooperate to find answers.

While huddles and meetings are beneficial for communicating updates to SOPs and other things, ideas for current issues can be generated at any moment. Managers must be approachable and have an open-door policy for effective deference to expertise. Consider a scenario where the boss is never seen, does not talk to anybody, and only shows up when something is wrong to ask questions. It is likely that the employees will be guarded, probably in fear of reprisal. When managers and other leadership roles in an organization are approachable, effective communication channels are open to allow individuals at all levels to engage in discussions, seek clarification, and share their perspectives.

Optimized Decision-Making

The responsibility for making strategic decisions that have a big or long-term impact on the company falls to the people in senior positions who have the appropriate knowledge and experience. On the other hand, people from all levels of the organization may participate in tactical decision-making, which focuses on the immediate actions needed to achieve long-term objectives. Organizations will need to balance which decisions are centralized with those that aren't. Operational decision-making must be left to the employees on the ground, with team-based decision-making that relies on consensus. These are the decisions that affect the daily operational tasks of the team, and enabling decision-making at the team level enables people to pitch in when there is a problem to solve.

High-tempo and high-risk situations need decentralized decision-making, and management should empower those on the frontline to make these decisions. For organizations that are data-driven, there is a need to integrate this data into the decision-making loop. The benefits are quality real time decisions and the ease of making these decisions. In the case of the Three Mile Nuclear incident, the operator was presented with ambiguous data, which was misleading. Had the indications been clear to signal what was actually happening, it is likely that the operator would have made decisions based on accurate data. Along with the ability to accurately determine what is going on, individuals with relevant expertise, regardless of their rank, must have the power to make decisions. This approach acknowledges the importance of specialized knowledge and ensures that decisions are made by those who are best equipped to handle the situation.

Bottom-up decision-making must be encouraged as much as possible, taking into account the issues involved and the areas of expertise along with the environment. The organization can gain from a variety of viewpoints, collective wisdom, and a feeling of ownership and empowerment among its members by allowing decisions to flow both ways.

Demonstrating Knowledge

Frontline employees and teams have to do their part for deference to expertise to be effective. There must be proactive action to share insights, and this begins with having a culture of continuous learning. A manager should keep track of and acknowledge employees who are continuously learning to deepen their knowledge either of the operations themselves or the industry in general. In addition to the demonstration of a willingness to contribute and actively participate, there must also be reliability at the individual level. Even when circumstances change, you must be able to deliver on your commitments. This can be combined with a positive attitude and a can-do approach. Individuals should strive to differentiate themselves from others by taking initiative and going above and beyond expectations. Managers should emphasize the value of this so that employees do not confuse this with competing with their peers but rather see it as a prompt to develop a reliable attitude at the individual level. When the people themselves are reliable, the organization can greatly improve its reliability. Seek opportunities to generate innovative solutions and deliver exceptional results. When you consistently demonstrate value through your unique contributions, management will be more open to exploring and testing your ideas.

Deference to Expertise Challenges

- **Lack of consensus:** A potential source of conflict is when there are multiple experts and different opinions, which makes it difficult to reach a consensus. Such cases make it difficult to decide whose opinion to defer to, especially when the possibilities are not clear-cut. Choosing a subset of experts based on personal preferences or desired outcomes can lead to biased decision-making. Another factor that adds to the complexity is the trustworthiness of the experts, which might not be easy to establish, particularly when the experts are not proven within the organization.

- **Autonomy vs. expert judgment:** People might think about forming views based on their own judgment if there isn't a clear expert agreement. In this regard, relying on experts may not always result in a clear-cut conclusion and may create a situation of uncertainty.

- **The complexity of the problem:** An expert in one field likely does not have expertise in another field, and when there is a problem that overlaps different fields, it may be difficult to defer to one expert or a group of them. The Challenger Disaster is an example of how a complex operation can have many experts with different objectives. The manufacturer of the shuttle clearly had economic experts who considered the consequences of delaying the launch and how their relationship with NASA would be soured if they listened to the engineers. Problems that have ripple effects are more difficult to solve if the group of experts in the room are not in agreement or willing to look at things from the perspective of other experts. In the end, one group of experts will get their way at the expense of others, and this can defeat the purpose of deferring to expertise.

Chapter 10

Sustaining Performance

G etting to the top is not so easy; staying there is more difficult. –Husnu Ozyegin

Building systems to adapt and recover when problems do occur is a result of understanding that no system is perfect. Failures will always happen, and the organization will need to adapt quickly to stay on top. Organizations work hard to achieve reliability status but work even harder to maintain it. Possible reasons for this include a changing business environment as well as complacency. The latter is undesirable because it means that the organization is going backward. We have already seen what happens when organizations forget the lessons of the past, in the case of Boeing and NASA. This is the reason high reliability depends on solid leadership with a commitment to keeping their organization an HRO. When the stakes are high, organizations seem to revert back to their old way of doing things. For instance, the 737 Max crisis was preceded by the two crashes of the earlier models of the aircraft in 1994, and in these cases, the company denied that there was anything wrong with the design. Hall and Goelz (2019) considered these to be the company's "stubborn resistance to admitting mistakes," which is a direct violation of the core expectation of the leadership in HROs discussed in Chapter 3. Remaining on top requires the same ingredients as building an HRO, and in this regard, proactivity is critical. When an organization proactively navigates the changing business environment with agility, it achieves sustained performance. This is done by staying true to the HRO mission and core values across time. It is essential that when the leadership changes, structures that ensure that the organization does not deviate from the established practices remain in place. The leadership should still remain accountable to the same principles, and for this, periodic audits are required as a guarantee.

A Case of the Birth and Death of an HRO

One example that can reveal how an organization can lose its reliability status over time is the case of Back Bay Children's Hospital Pediatric Intensive Care Unit (PICU). For 11 years, the medical institution enjoyed a high-reliability status, which had been built around the employees. Prior to implementing HRO principles, the unit experienced double the mortality rate for children transported to the hospital compared to children admitted directly from another department within the institution. After several incidents in 1991 and 1993 resulting in deterioration and deaths during transport, changes were made using HRO principles. Children with potential airway instability would have a tube inserted in the windpipe before leaving the referring facility. Other changes included a clinical respiratory examination replacing the traditional blood gas measurements and chest radiographs (Roberts et al., 2005). These measures, along with other HRO-oriented interventions, curbed health deterioration during transport, and for one year, there were no mortalities associated with complications during transport.

When compared to other intensive care units within the facility, the PICU had a greater ratio of long-term personnel, with attrition at roughly 5%. The PICU's collaboration and goal-directed team formation were prioritized over hierarchical duties in order to support the bedside caregiver. The PICU adopted a variety of treatment strategies developed from problem-solving techniques while avoiding blame and shame. Caregivers were free to attempt different therapies, and open discussion of issues was encouraged. Each caregiver was valued as a long-term team member, and shortcomings in care were seen as teaching opportunities.

Road to HRO

The specific HRO activities implemented were:

- **Risk perception:** Early on in the PICU's establishment, risk awareness presented a problem. Children frequently appeared physically stable as the team achieved control over acute sickness or injury, leading to a perception of healing rather than detecting hidden risks. To combat this, in-service seminars tailored to understanding the progression of child illness were implemented. Additionally, regular seminars were arranged for the nurses working in intensive care units and emergency departments. By 1997, unanticipated patient deterioration in the PICU had become infrequent, and patient deterioration in the hospital ward had become rare. Few patients—if any—needed to be readmitted to the PICU after being discharged.

- **Command and control:** The PICU was

successful because command and control were crucial components of care. It was now up to the team member with the best qualifications to make decisions. With their close proximity to patients, bedside caregivers frequently made immediate decisions depending on treatment outcomes, providing stability in constantly changing circumstances. These reactions helped with diagnosis and guided subsequent treatment. There was no such thing as a bad choice because each one led to new information that was useful for treating patients. Professional engagement forms were designed to alleviate the authority gap between doctors and other team members. Through the use of these forms, the nursing staff was able to pass concerns and recommendations on to the relevant physician. This strategy eliminated hostility and intimidation, safeguarded nurses from retaliation, and promoted cooperation.

- **Process auditing:** The practice of critical care medicine took place in a volatile and uncertain setting. The staff actively looked for areas that could be improved, and they promoted discussion and the presenting of data to back or oppose their theories. Any team member was able to raise concerns about patient care, which immediately changed how the patient was treated.

- **Quality management:** To guarantee that the PICU maintained the lowest rate of potentially avoidable mortality and morbidity, regular quality evaluations were carried out. These reviews were carried out as quickly as possible following an incident, promoting close communication between attending doctors and caregivers at the bedside. When an incident caused serious harm, quality improvement procedures were put in place, and the government got involved to help resolve problems. The quality reference levels for improvement were informed by national standards and pertinent medical literature.

- **Process redundancy:** To guarantee thorough patient evaluation and treatment selection, redundancy was used. Critical signs were tracked using a variety of techniques, and during resuscitations, various team members kept an eye on the same vital signs. By putting standards and procedures into place, respiratory care practitioners (RCPs) and nurses were given more power over patient care and could react to changes more quickly. Therapist-driven protocols provide an organized approach by taking into account the patient's prior experiences and anticipated responses.

- **Reward systems:** A rewards system was in place to encourage active involvement in patient care. Rewards and recognition were frequently given on an internal basis to team members who had shown knowledge, judgment, and insight. Their perspectives were sought out and included in care plans, and those people had a bigger impact on tactical and strategic management. All disciplines were involved, and the goals were to reduce accidents and stress while boosting caregiver morale.

Changes Affecting HRO Principles

Changes in human resources initiated the departure from HRO practices in the unit. Two leading advocates for HRO, who were senior physicians with the unit, left the organization one after the other, and their replacements were several ICU-attending physicians, which increased the staff to six experts with two fellows. Within the same period, the responsibilities of the unit increased as cardiothoracic surgeons were added to the department, along with the addition of sedation interventions.

At first, only the physician culture transitioned from the HRO to the traditional medical model. Nursing and RCP actions continued to be in line with earlier developed HRO practices but were occasionally faced with fierce opposition. This led to attrition and consequently led to new grads being hired in the PICU without having completed the previously required one year of ICU experience.

The operations themselves changed as well. RCPs were no longer allowed to suggest treatments, and some faced criticism for making any suggestions. On the front, the attending staff began to provide support increasingly through telephone consultations and distant evaluations. Bedside staff felt unsupported when dealing with unstable or deteriorating patients. Refusal of ICU transfer requests caused confusion among physicians in the hospital and community who were accustomed to the previous HRO model where the indication for PICU admission was the request by a physician. Slowly, patients discharged from the PICU started to be readmitted within 48 hours, a clear indication that reliability status had been lost.

Regardless of the indications, nothing was done, and part of the reason is that the remaining staff lacked experience. This led to a return to a medical model where the physician assumed leadership. As a result, teams were formed based on status and role, a clear departure from the principle of deference to expertise. Protocols and algorithms were followed for safety, and central authority was maintained by the physician. Treatment of critically ill patients relies on evidence-based medicine. The previous HRO model of decision migration was deemed unsafe. Loop decision-making techniques like the Boyd OODA loop discussed earlier were rejected as unfamiliar and confusing. From this, we can draw several important lessons that HROs need to be mindful of if they need to maintain HRO status.

Pillars of Sustained Performance

Commitment to Value-Based Operations

Proven organizational culture should not be allowed to change when the leadership changes. You can consider a nation: When new leadership comes in, the constitution remains in place unless amended through the set processes. Policies can be improved as things change, but HRO practices must never be discarded. In the aftermath of the 737

Max crashes, a lot of employees came forward in an attempt to shed light on what was actually going on behind the scenes. The culture of "Working Together" established in the days of former CEO Mulally no longer existed, and some employees pointed out that they saw the company change right before their eyes. One of the interviewees boldly claimed that "Boeing quit listening to their employees. Every time I'd raise my hand and say, hey we got a problem here, they would attack the messenger and ignore the message" (Marshall Goldsmith, n.d.). Some claimed that their pay was affected if they put quality concerns in writing. Soon, most people fell in line and refrained from raising any issues, and this set the stage for the 737 Max crisis and the other challenges with reliability the plane maker faced on its other models. When implementing a pro-HRO culture, make sure that you create a structure that makes it difficult for people to change secretly, even after the pioneers have left the organization. This is where leadership transparency takes center stage, which in itself acts as a deterrent to cutting corners and abuse of power.

The converse is also true. Lessons learned will soon be lost if employees lose sight of how organizational goals relate to their daily tasks and what is actually required of them. Managers on the ground must uphold order and consistency. If a culture of "letting things slide" takes hold, the quality of work suffers, which in turn leads to a culture of cutting corners. Employees need to commit daily and take ownership of the work, matching this with the organization's priorities.

Resilient Leadership

People always look up to their leadership regardless of the phase an organization is going through. When a company is going through a crisis, it is essential that the leadership remains resilient and assures the rest of the team that they can navigate the crisis. One important characteristic of resilience is innate adaptation to change. Even when all the pieces are not in place, resilient leaders are quick to recognize change and embrace it as an opportunity for growth. They encourage agility and adaptability within the organization, enabling it to respond effectively to emerging challenges and uncertainties. This promotes a flexible mindset that encourages innovation and thinking outside the box.

Resilient Teams

HROs have low attrition rates. Experienced professionals are needed in the field to act as custodians of good engineering practices that recent graduates might not necessarily have. In this regard, they will act as teachers, and this way, the culture of reliability is maintained. A leading cause of the loss of HRO status for Back Bay Children's Hospital was the introduction of a significant number of inexperienced personnel, meaning no one really had enough experience working in an ICU. Maintain a balance between fresh theoretical knowledge and knowledge gained over time. Remuneration needs to be competitive and the working conditions attractive to keep employees interested in giving their best and staying with the organization. This must also be matched with performance because people do not automatically perform at a high level throughout time. Individuals must be periodically evaluated and given specialized skill development and training so that they keep performing at their best level. Resilient teams:

- **Plan for work:** Clear goals and expectations are essential to the success of resilient teams. Setting realistic yet demanding goals that are in line with the objectives of the organization, resilient leaders work together with team members to plan work successfully.

- **Perform self-assessments:** To spot possible problems and growth opportunities, teams need the ability to continuously assess their performance on their own before managers get to sit down with teams and discuss how things are going. When work is measured by the individual, personal goals towards improvement can be set, and managers can complement this by offering assistance and direction as required. This allows members to benefit from coaching and mentorship to build capacity.

It is clear that for an HRO to remain so, there must be a continued commitment to the principles we have discussed because that is what sustains performance. The cycle must remain intact, and organizations must reevaluate and adjust, refining what works and discarding what does not.

Conclusion

While this book is tailored mainly towards engineering professionals in managerial positions within high-risk operations, frontline employees and graduates seeking reliable operations can also benefit. Unreliability affects the organization as a whole, and at times, individual careers can be destroyed, as revealed by the case studies looked at. The Three Mile Nuclear Incident, the Challenger Disaster, and the Bhopal Chemical Leak are known examples of unwanted outcomes when an organization lacks a framework for reliability. The way things are being done is evolving, and the demand for HROs is growing beyond the traditional large-scale, high-risk operations such as a huge nuclear plant. Other industries, such as banks and hospitals, have incorporated reliability into their operations.

Most complex operations can be transformed into high-reliability operations. The secret is to tailor the application of the five principles anchoring HROs to achieve safety, resilience, and efficient risk management learned from organizations that have achieved such. Even in the face of uncertainty and unforeseen events, these organizations have continuously produced outcomes that are trustworthy and safe. A cultural shift is the foundation that paves the way for people to understand the five principles, and fostering the change in culture requires starting from the basics of a strong safety culture, open communication, employee empowerment, and ongoing learning and development. This is a mindset that each participant in the organization needs to develop. The idea of HROs recognizes that mistakes and accidents are not completely avoidable but instead focuses on creating practices and systems that can identify risks and reduce them before they become more serious. Reinventing an organization into an HRO places priority on spotting possible risks and anomalies quickly, followed by prompt action to prevent negative outcomes.

Interlocking the desired reliability and the actions to operationalize this reliability is the "organizational mindset." The needed mindset is different across the organizational structure. For executives, risks inherent to the business must be acknowledged and errors contextualized. Overall, executives must be responsible for system issues that can be proactively solved through model-based approaches. On the other hand, managers need to leverage problem-solving and make effective improvements in how problems are solved. Managers serve as the link between the goal of the organization and the frontline employees. When the mindset is right, it becomes fertile ground for the cultural or behavioral change needed to operationalize reliability. Before the training and exercises targeting the mindset, a baseline must be defined to set the minimum behavior expectations for the whole organization. Managers can use this baseline to check the progress and work to correct deviations from the expected culture and behavior. Only when teams have developed a culture of reliability can they truly begin to implement the principles of HROs.

The first and perhaps most important principle is **preoccupation with failure**. Situational awareness, anticipation of potential outcomes, and persistent investigation into unknown causes of failure are core skills needed to develop an organization that is preoccupied with failure. The benefits are enhanced risk management, vigilance, and innovation. However, teams must be careful when preoccupied with failure because if unchecked, there is a risk of fixation on minor issues at the expense of the bigger picture. Communication lines must be open and clear, with individuals being encouraged to be proactive in addressing issues. Overall, preoccupation with failure encourages continuous attention to anomalies and acknowledges the limitations of knowledge in uncovering potential issues.

Next is the **reluctance to simplify**, and the emphasis is on persistence when it comes to analyzing failures and avoiding oversimplified explanations. When an incident occurs, priority must be placed on thorough investigation over quick conclusions. The airline industry's meticulous examination of aircraft incidents exemplifies this principle. HROs assemble multidisciplinary teams to address complex issues, fostering diverse perspectives and minimizing simplification. Such teams prevent hidden factors from causing unreliability and ensure all aspects of a problem are considered. When multidisciplinary teams are involved, problem-solving is improved by incorporating varied expertise, ensuring equitable communication, and identifying blind spots. Hypotheses and scientific tools like Failure Mode and Effects Analysis (FMEA) and Root Cause Analysis (RCA) aid teams in accurate problem identification. However, excessive reluctance to simplify can lead to overcomplication, hinder resource allocation, and impede coordination. Striking a balance between comprehensive analysis and practical action is vital, as excessive complexity can result in missed crucial information.

Organizations must prioritize optimal solutions while avoiding resource wastage.

The third principle upon which HROs are built is **sensitivity to operations**. In this regard, the emphasis is on the **consequences of human error**, commitment to individual and team resilience, process simplification, reduced autonomy, and highlighting deviations from practice. Scenario planning is the core competence here, and HROs stand out for their ability to quickly contain faults, continue operations despite setbacks, and respond effectively to system failures. Simplifying processes reduces cognitive load, enhances comprehension, and minimizes errors, contributing to organizational resilience. Reducing autonomy promotes adherence to best practices, while deviations from established procedures are valuable when well-recorded for future improvements. The concept of Layer of Protection Analysis (LOPA) identifies weaknesses in systems and adds layers of protection to enhance resilience. Scenario planning assesses risks and possibilities, guiding standardization efforts to respond effectively to failures. Organizational fluidity is needed and can be achieved through strong social networks and adaptable structures. This empowers HROs to swiftly react to internal and external pressures.

Another feature of HROs is that knowledge is valued regardless of where it is coming from. This is **deference to expertise** and requires the organization as a whole to be accountable and own the problem or solution. This ownership and accountability focuses on solving problems rather than playing politics based on seniority. Transparency in decision-making is crucial. Making the decision-making process visible and explaining rationale builds confidence, encourages employees to share thoughts, and promotes collaboration across hierarchies.

When all this has been nurtured, resilience is the ultimate achievement, and organizations are guaranteed sustained performance, which is the capstone of HROs. It is critical for daily tasks and organizational goals to be aligned so that quality is maintained. Resilient leadership is a must during a crisis, and leaders can demonstrate this by being adaptive, innovative, and agile. Teams with high levels of resilience in HROs are known to hold on to seasoned workers who provide crucial knowledge while balancing theoretical understanding and real-world experience. For HROs to maintain high performance, there must be clear goals, continuous self-assessment, and individualized improvement plans. A steadfast commitment to all the principles of HROs sustains HRO performance with a requirement of ongoing evaluation, adaptation, and refinement. With these principles, any dedicated professional can drive the transformation of their organization into a high-reliability organization.

Ace Your STEM Interviews with Proven Strategies

STEM Success with Proven Strategies

About the Author

Jeffrey Harvey's over 30 years as a professional engineer in STEM positions grants him unique expertise to answer questions young STEM professionals face. The STEM field is ever-growing, and the need for professionals has never been higher, so helping a whole new generation succeed has become one of Jeffrey's driving forces. As a father to three boys—all with STEM-related fields of study and work—and as a professional, he understands the struggles of this new wave that young professionals face.

Originally from Wyoming, Jeffrey resides in Oklahoma with his lovely wife, two step-children, and their Basenji dog. In his downtime, he enjoys being outdoors, writing books, remodeling, reading, traveling, and learning about other cultures. His extensive experience in different leadership positions, including Engineering Director, several positions as an Engineering Manager, accounting-related supervisor, Project Manager for major and minor projects leading all disciplines, and different individual contributor engineering and STEM roles for two Fortune 500 companies, make him a multi-faceted expert that can help any professional achieve their dreams.

www.jeffreyharveype.com

LinkedIn
https://www.linkedin.com/in/jeffreyharveype/

Instagram
https://www.instagram.com/jeffreyharveype/

Facebook
https://www.facebook.com/jeffreyharveype/

Twitter
https://twitter.com/jeffreyharveype

Pinterest
https://www.pinterest.com/jeffreyharveype/

References

Berkes, H. (2016, March 21). *Challenger engineer who warned of shuttle disaster dies*. The Two Way. https://www.npr.org/sections/thetwo-way/2016/03/21/470870426/challenger-engineer-who-warned-of-shuttle-disaster-dies

Clarke, D. (2008). Managing the Unexpected: Resilient Performance in an Age of Uncertainty (2nd edn) Karl E Weick and Kathleen M Sutcliffe (2007) Wiley & Sons, San Francisco. *Journal of Management & Organization, 14*(5), 593–594. https://doi.org/10.1017/S1833367200003072

Clayton, M. (2021, August 1). *Max Verstappen battles back for 2 precious points in Hungary*. Red Bull. https://www.redbull.com/int-en/hungary-f1-grand-prix-2021-race-report

Crail, C. & Lupini, C. (2021, July 5). *Boeing 737 MAX: What is safety, anyway?* Forbes.

https://www.forbes.com/advisor/credit-cards/trav
el-rewards/737-max-what-is-safety-anyway/

Crawford, J. (2023). *Leadership–advancing great leaders and leadership*. IntechOpen. https://doi.org/10.5772/intechopen.104266

Curtis, J. & Gill, J. (2022, November 11). *Potential UK support for investigations into the Bhopal gas explosion*. House of Commons Library. https://commonslibrary.parliament.uk/research-br iefings/cdp-2022-0202/

DEKRA. (2021, March 3). *Operationalizing the characteristics of high-reliability organizations.* https://www.dekrasafetyblog.com/high-reliability-organizations

Dobrijevic, D. & Howell, E. (2023, January 25). *Columbia disaster: What happened and what NASA learned.* Space.com. https://www.space.com/19436-columbia-disaster.html

Fallon, N. (2023, February 21). *25 inspiring leadership quotes.* Business News Daily. https://www.businessnewsdaily.com/7481-leadersh ip-quotes.html

Federal Aviation Administration (2022, December 19). *McDonnell Douglas D-10.* United States

Department of Transportation. https://www.faa.gov/lessons_learned/transport_ai rplane/accidents/N1819U

Ferrazzi, K., Race, M., & Vincent, A. (2021, January 21). *7 strategies to build a more resilient team*. Harvard Business Review. https://hbr.org/2021/01/7-strategies-to-build-a-mo re-resilient-team

Freundlich, R. E., Bulka, C. M., Wanderer, J. P., Rothman, B. S., Sandberg, W. S., & Ehrenfeld, J. M. (2020). Prospective investigation of the operating room time-out process. *Anesthesia and analgesia, 130*(3), 725–729. https://doi.org/10.1213/ANE.0000000000004126

Gaunt, M. J. (2019, June 22). *Safety requires a healthy preoccupation with failure*. Pharmacy Times. https://www.pharmacytimes.com/view/safety-req uires-a-healthy-preoccupation-with-failure

German vs Japanese Cars: Which one to buy? (n.d.). Al-Futtaim Automall. https://www.automalluae.com/en/news/german-vs -japanese-cars-which-one-to-buy/

Goswami, D. (2019, January 17). *How did the real Sully pull off miracle landing of Flight 1549? Hear it from the Captain himself.* India Today.

https://www.indiatoday.in/trending-news/story/captain-chesley-sully-sullenberger-miracle-on-hudson-landing-tweets-1432338-2019-01-16

Grabowski, M., & Roberts, K. H. (2019). Reliability seeking virtual organizations: Challenges for high reliability organizations and resilience engineering. *Safety Science*, *117*, 512–522. https://doi.org/10.1016/j.ssci.2016.02.016

Green, P. (2022, November 26). *United Airlines Flight 232—a cabin crew perspective.* Simple Flying. https://simpleflying.com/united-airlines-flight-232-a-cabin-crew-perspective/

G, A. (2022, May 25). *Who makes the most reliable German cars?* Car Vertical. https://www.carvertical.com/blog/who-makes-the-most-reliable-german-cars

Hall, J., & Goelz, P. (2019, July 17). *The Boeing 737 Max crisis is a leadership failure.* The New York Times. https://www.nytimes.com/2019/07/17/opinion/boeing-737-max.html

Hviid, J. (2021, June 30). *NAT and HRO; summary.* ROC Consult. https://rocconsult.eu/nat-and-hro-summary/

Iorio, S. (2021, September 23). *What the HRO trait "preoccupation with failure" looks like in practice + free tools*. American Data Network. https://www.americandatanetwork.com/patient-sa fety/what-the-hro-trait-preoccupation-with-failur e-looks-like-in-practice-free-tools/

Jurecko, L. (2021, March 16). *10 leadership mindsets for high reliability organizations*. Cleveland Clinic. https://consultqd.clevelandclinic.org/10-leadership -mindsets-for-high-reliability-organizations/

Krasnopevtseva, N. J., Thomas, C., & Kaminska, R. (2019). *The dynamics of safety risk perception in high reliability organizations*. https://doi.org/10.3850/978-981-14-8593-0_4147-c d

Landry, L. (2020, March 5). *Why managers should involve their team in the decision-making process.* Harvard Business School. https://online.hbs.edu/blog/post/team-decision-m aking

Marshall Goldsmith. (n.d.). *The downfall Of Boeing: The deathly impact of bad leadership & toxic culture*. https://knowledgebank.mgscc.net/the-downfall-of -boeing-the-deathly-impact-of-bad-leadership-to xic-culture

National Transportation Safety Board. (n.d.). *Marine accident brief.* https://www.ntsb.gov/investigations/AccidentRepo rts/Reports/MAB0501.pdf

9 safety at work quotes to promote risk reduction. (2022, January 17). Rescu. https://www.rescusaveslives.com/blog/9-safety-at-work-quotes-to-promote-risk-reduction/

Nolan, D. P. (2019). *Handbook of fire and explosion protection engineering principles for oil, gas, chemical and related facilities.* https://www.sciencedirect.com/book/9780128160 022/handbook-of-fire-and-explosion-protection-engineering-principles-for-oil-gas-chemical-and-related-facilities

Norris-Tull, D. (n.d.). *History: Are we doomed to repeat it?* Management of Invasive Plants in The Western USA. https://www.invasiveplantswesternusa.org/history-are-we-doomed-to-repeat-it.html

Perrow, C. (1999). *Normal accidents: Living with high risk technologies.* Princeton University Press.

Pigford, T. H. (1981). The Management of Nuclear Safety: Lessons Learned from the Accident at Three Mile Island. *Nuclear Engineering for an Uncertain Future,* 89–102.

https://link.springer.com/chapter/10.1007/978-1-4684-4184-0_6

Pool, R. (1997). *Beyond engineering: How society shapes technology*. Oxford University Press.

Predictive maintenance. (n.d.). General Electric. https://www.ge.com/research/project/predictive-maintenance

Pyke, T. (2020a, November 9). *How do we commit to resilience?* High Reliability Organizing. https://www.high-reliability.org/how-do-we-commit-to-resilience

Pyke, T. (2020b, November 9). *Sensitivity to operations II*. High Reliability Organizing. https://www.high-reliability.org/sensitivity-to-operations-ii

Roberts, K. H. (2003). *HRO has prominent history*. Anesthesia Patient Safety Foundation. https://www.apsf.org/article/hro-has-prominent-history

Roberts, K. H., Madsen, P., Desai, V., & Van Stralen, D. (2005). A case of the birth and death of a high reliability healthcare organisation. *BMJ Quality & Safety*, *14*(3), 216–220. https://doi.org/10.1136/qshc.2003.009589

Roth, B. M., & Mullen, J. D. (2002). *Decision making: Its logic and practice.* Rowman & Littlefield.

Sadek, N. (2022, October 11). *Boeing whistleblower's journey from pre-crash warnings, to going public in their wake.* International Consortium of Investigative Journalists. https://www.icij.org/inside-icij/2022/10/its-like-a-rollercoaster-boeing-whistleblowers-journey-from-pre-crash-warnings-to-going-public-in-their-wake/

Sibilski, P. (2020). *Safety layers and layer of protection analysis (LOPA).* AIChE. https://www.aiche.org/sites/default/files/community/206296/aiche-community-site-files/2979826/safetylayersinbhopal-compatibilitymode.pdf

Snyder, M. (2018). *Building the high-reliability organization (HRO): Measuring and managing the four critical disciplines that produce consistent safety outcomes.* DEKRA. https://www.dekra.us/en/organizational-safety-reliability/content-page-158/

Snyder, M. (2021, September 24). *The 5 disciplines of high-reliability organizations.* EHS Today. https://www.ehstoday.com/safety-leadership/article/21176403/the-5-disciplines-of-highreliability-organizations

Thomas, L. (2007, December 14). *A new breed of billionaire*. New York Times. https://www.nytimes.com/2007/12/14/business/14billionaire.html#:~:text=%E2%80%9CI'm%20first%20generation%2C,days%20of%20the%20Ottoman%20Empire.

Tikkanen, A. (2023, September 11). *Titanic*. Encyclopedia Britannica. https://www.britannica.com/topic/Titanic

Tsukayama, H. (2018, February 23). *How Samsung moved beyond its exploding phones*. The Washington Post. https://www.washingtonpost.com/business/how-samsung-moved-beyond-its-exploding-phones/2018/02/23/5675632c-182f-11e8-b681-2d4d462a1921_story.html

Turbli (2022, January 10). *The safest transport modes, ranked by statistics from 10 years of data*. https://turbli.com/blog/the-safest-transport-modes-ranked-by-statistics-from-10-years-of-data/

United States Nuclear Regulatory Commission. (2022, November 15). *Backgrounder on the Three Mile Island accident*. https://www.nrc.gov/reading-rm/doc-collections/fact-sheets/3mile-isle.html

van Stralen, D., & Mercer, T. A. (2021). High-Reliability Organizing (HRO), Decision Making, the OODA Loop, and COVID-19. *Neonatology Today*, *16*. https://doi.org/10.51362/neonatology.today/202141 6490101

VanderMey, J. (2020, November 5). *Normalization of deviance: Definition, examples and solutions.* O   S   T   . https://www.ostusa.com/blog/normalization-of-de viance-definition-examples-and-solutions/

Veterans Benefits Information. (2016). *HRO corner: Delving into the reluctance to simplify high reliability organization guiding principle.* http://veteransbenefitsinformation.com/latest-new s/10685-hro-corner-delving-into-thereluctance-t o-simplify-high-reliability-organization-guiding-p rinciple.html

Vogus, T. J., & Rerup, C. (2018). Sweating the "small stuff": High-reliability organizing as a foundation for sustained superior performance. *Strategic Organization*, *16*(2), 227–238. https://www.jstor.org/stable/26506126

Ware, D. G. (2016, January 28). *Engineer who warned of 1986 Challenger disaster still racked with guilt, three decades on.* United Press I   n   t   e   r   n   a   t   i   o   n   a   l   .

https://www.upi.com/Top_News/US/2016/01/28/E
ngineer-who-warned-of-1986-Challenger-disaster
-still-racked-with-guilt-three-decades-on/489145
4032643/

Weick, K. E., & Sutcliffe, K. M. (2015). *Managing the
unexpected: Sustained performance in a complex
world.* John Wiley & Sons.

World Nuclear Association. (2022, April). *Three
Mile Island accident.*
https://world-nuclear.org/information-library/safe
ty-and-security/safety-of-plants/three-mile-island
-accident.aspx

Worsnip, Alex (n.d.). *Deference to Experts.*
https://www.alexworsnip.com/wp-content/upload
s/2023/01/Deference-to-Experts.pdf.

Zadeh, M. M. (2022, October 1). *An
introduction to high-reliability leadership
style in healthcare.* Intech Open.
https://www.intechopen.com/chapters/83945